The Three Paradoxes of
Roland Barthes

The Three Paradoxes of

Roland Barthes

Patrizia Lombardo

The University of Georgia Press

Athens and London

Visual Studies Workshop
Research Center
Rochester, N.Y.
SUNY Brockport
July 1991

© 1989 by the University of Georgia Press
Athens, Georgia 30602
All rights reserved
Designed by Mary Mendell
Set in Pilgrim
The paper in this book meets the guidelines for permanence
and durability of the Committee on Production Guidelines for
Book Longevity of the Council on Library Resources.
Printed in the United States of America
93 92 91 90 89   5 4 3 2 1
Library of Congress Cataloging in Publication Data
Lombardo, Patrizia.
  The three paradoxes of Roland Barthes/Patrizia Lombardo.
    p.   cm.
  Bibliography: p.
  Includes index.
  ISBN 0-8203-1139-1 (alk. paper)
    1. Barthes, Roland. I. Title.
P85.B33L66 1989
808'.00141—dc19   88-39328
                                                  CIP

British Library Cataloging in Publication Data available

Contents

One cannot undertake the study of any author without asking oneself what, after all, *is* criticism—a question that becomes all the more urgent when the author studied is a critic. One would like a firm, trustworthy answer to use as a point of departure, if not also as a point of arrival. There is, of course, no definitive answer because literary criticism is centered on that very question, which has as its double another question that directs and orients it: what is literature? But literature simply *is*—and has been, and will be.

It was through this process of questioning without finding an answer that I decided to begin my study with *Writing Degree Zero*, in which Barthes, at the beginning of his critical enterprise, sought to define literature and formulated his notion of *writing*.

When I write, problems become gradually very concrete. At some point, after the initial decision of a subject or a theme, I realize that the pages are multiplying and the argument is proceeding by a weaving together of ideas and fragments: the luminous citations of a text or an author, sentences that strike me by their music or because they make up essential links in a chain of argumentation. I am not sure what comes first, the idea of a critical interpretation or these flashes. It really matters little: this is the only time when I believe that it is possible for reading and writing to coincide and that such a coincidence can exist alongside the deep divergence between reading and writing, before the decision to write actually takes place, before the *vouloir-écrire* comes into being.

Roland Barthes: my debt toward him lies in this will-to-write. I owe him neither a method nor a set of concepts—I could have found both elsewhere—but an attitude, a moral sense. Not knowledge, but will. In "Inaugural Lecture," Barthes said: "*Sapientia:* no power, a little knowledge, a little wisdom, and as much flavor as possible."[1]

Roland Barthes: my maestro. I like using that outmoded name. I can see him still—in the seminar, rue de Tournon in Paris, where a few years ago, on the occasion of an exhibit on the Viennese architect Adolf Loos, I visited again the place, now changed into a gallery, where we used to meet in a small group. The ecstasy of the seminar, which Barthes himself had commented on so many times—the religion of friendship, the religion of literature.

I remember Roland Barthes in New York, in October or November 1978, at New York University, in an immense and overcrowded auditorium. He spoke of Proust and his own intention to write a novel of *pathos*. It was an unexpected lecture, altogether unwonted, the way prophecies today are unexpected and unwonted—or even personal declarations, when they are devoid of sentimentality, for we have become so accustomed to professionalism and coded languages.

That room and his voice: combined images of his success and his solitude, his slightly bashful being. I did not listen to what might be called a good lecture, a good academic performance, but I experienced the space, time, and accent of true words.

It was not my intention to write an homage to Barthes. Nor was it my intention to write a comprehensive study on Barthes and structuralism, or any other intellectual movement (there are already several studies of this type, and two of them are remarkable: by Annette Lavers and Steven Ungar). I wanted to focus on what I consider the most original quality of Barthes within our contemporary literature and criticism, which is simply his concern for literature and its destiny in a world where there is very little place for it. This is the reason why I do not follow the chronology, or deal with all his books. I insist on some and neglect others, even if they are the most famous ones that launched a new approach in literary studies (like *On Racine* and *S/Z*). I am not primarily interested in Barthes's structuralism or semiotics, in the avant-garde pretensions of the new. I would say that I am more interested in the failure of structuralism, in Barthes's invalidation of the scientific dream of the 1960s and 1970s. I think that it is worthwhile today to stress the genealogy of literary thought that obviously links Barthes to several nineteenth-century French writers and Proust, and almost unexpectedly to writers like Hugo von Hofmannsthal, who, at the turn of the century, gave voice to a deep historical crisis and his personal melancholy in a world lapsing away. I see Barthes as part of this crucial ambiguity that determined the modern writer, or the writer of modernity, since Baudelaire and Flaubert. This ambiguity consists in an irresistible attraction for something new, different, breaking with the past, and at the same time an unavoidable scorn for the contemporary world, all the empty talk that gives us the illusion that we belong to something.

I want to trace the pattern of that ambiguity, which is formal as well as political. Barthes oscillated between a revolutionary position and a reactionary one, between the rhetoric of the new and the inclination toward the past. I pursue the paradoxes which make their way throughout Barthes's career. Not to pass judgment. Is the paradox not itself, to speak like Barthes, an affective figure? To signal a paradox in the writers we love, the sentences we are fascinated by, means to save them from public opinion, from the *doxa*. It is sheltering words from their circulation, their degradation, from the fixedness of labels, which are always reductive, even when they are necessary in order to come to some basic understanding. We are constantly torn between the need to simplify—to make things clear—and the sense that things are extremely subtle, complex, delicate. To observe paradoxes means to be aware that language is altogether too poor and too rich. Contradictions, as Blanchot said, are "the reality of the literary effort."[2]

The first paradox, which I discuss in chapter 1, is related to a commonplace that seems to cling to the reception of structuralism: the assumption that historicism and formalism are opposites. I believe on the contrary that, since the beginning of his critical enterprise, Barthes was concerned with historical problems, almost obsessed with them. For this reason, I consider that *Writing Degree Zero*, although it is an early work, remains fundamental to the understanding of his particular formalism. His first book already contained all the most important themes of Barthes's subsequent research on the relationship between a writer and history, understood both as his own time and as the history of literature. I will also stress the importance of one of his less-appreciated books, almost contemporary with *Writing Degree Zero*, his *Michelet*, which was translated into English only in 1987. Strangely enough, in the very years Barthes started to be interested in structuralist linguistics, he devoted a monograph to the nineteenth-century historian. Later, I will try to identify the implications of his continuous interest in Michelet, up to his last book, *Camera Lucida*, which I will deal with in chapter 3. The tension between literature and history opens up to a problem of representation, which haunted Barthes as much as our entire generation. The interest in photography is a further step in the analysis of this same problem.

I define Barthes's second paradox with a blunt statement, which is the title of chapter 2: "Against Language." These words theatrically challenge the most widespread stereotype of the structuralist and post-structuralist age, namely, that everything is language. My effort in this chapter is to weave together the different and often contradictory positions Barthes adopted regarding language. In this respect, one should insist on his 1978 inaugural lecture at the Collège de France, and what I would call the critical tragedy, the burning paradox it represented: in the very moment Barthes was giving status to the new discipline of "semiology," he publicly rejected its scientific pretensions, proclaimed the "fascism" of language, and expressed his nostalgic love for literature, in terms close to Proust's aesthetics.

In chapter 3, the discussion of Barthes's hesitations as regards realism brings us back again to the rapport between him and Proust, so obvious in *Camera Lucida*. However, I think that Barthes's author, his great passion, the one he identified with, was less Proust than Michelet, who, standing alone and resolute against his own century, spoke of love. With Michelet the tension between history and literature, which opened my investigation, comes back as a conclusion. In spite of the expectations Barthes himself created with all his talk about his desire to write a novel, I consider *Camera Lucida* the only novel he "could" write, and, maybe, he wanted to write: an essay, in which the critical analysis of photography and the meditation on time and death perfectly blend in a very personal research.

My ideal for critical writing: it should be simultaneously lucid, capable of mastering knowledge and constructing an argument, and intense, able to be moved, to let its own emotion come through (one might say that it should have the force of a statement as well as that of an utterance). It should be as clear and balanced as classical architecture while permitting Delacroix's colorism. It should echo and incorporate into itself the *libido* behind thought, explanation, and feeling. Couldn't this be the definition of the *essay*, that very form Barthes produced at the end of his life and that, I believe, will remain, beyond the fragility of intellectual fashions, as one of the most interesting and beautiful literary expressions of the last twenty years?

Acknowledgments

Part of chapter 2 was published in an earlier version under the title "Contre le langage" in *Critique* 423–24 (August–September 1982):726–33; part of chapter 3 was published under the title "Le Dernier Livre" in *L'Esprit créateur* 22 (Spring 1982):79–87. I wish to thank the editors of these journals, both for publishing those pages and for permission to reuse the material.

Invitations to lecture and valuable discussions helped me to clarify my ideas, in particular at University of Venice Ca' Foscari, Amsterdam Free University, New York University, Louisiana State University, University of California (Santa Cruz and Berkeley), and Wake Forest University. Two graduate seminars, at Princeton University in 1983 and at the University of Southern California in 1987, were important experiences on the way to this book.

I am profoundly grateful to Jessica Levine, who aptly translated a first draft of my manuscript from the Italian. Timothy Hampton helped with this translation. Nathaniel Wing and Jefferson Humphries encouraged me to submit my manuscript to the University of Georgia Press. François Wahl, Daniel Russell, and Antoine Compagnon read successive versions of this book with care and strictness. It is a pleasure to acknowledge what I owe to their criticisms.

**The Three Paradoxes of
Roland Barthes**

1 History and Form

Que livres, écrits, langage soient destinés à des métamorphoses auxquelles s'ouvrent déjà, à notre insu, nos habitudes, mais se refusent encore nos traditions; que les bibliothèques nous impressionnent par leur apparence d'autre monde, comme si, là, avec curiosité, étonnement et respect, nous découvrions tout à coup, après un voyage cosmique, les vestiges d'une autre planète plus ancienne, figée dans l'éternité du silence, il faudrait être bien peu familier avec soi pour ne pas s'en apercevoir.—Maurice Blanchot, *Le Livre à venir*

The Price of Form

One cannot dissolve the bond between language and our history, understood as hubris of the present, that something hanging in the air like a more or less obscure necessity, a mass of myths, utopias, systems, trends. Such a bond is indissoluble and double: simultaneously affiliation and revolt, opposition and complicity, a sense of belonging and the desire to keep one's distance. At first, and for good reason, *Writing Degree Zero* seems a work that exists entirely in an existentialist, Sartrean atmosphere. One only has to consider the title of the first essay in the collection, "What Is Writing?" which echoes the famous title of Sartre's *What is Literature?* or the recurrence of the terms and themes of liberty and responsibility. Read with the wisdom of hindsight and the insights of Saussurian semiology, *Writing Degree Zero* seems to anticipate and introduce linguistic structuralism in literary criticism: "The fact that the dialectics of language and speech are the very foundation of *Degree Zero* has not been recognized."[1] Such is Annette Lavers's comment in *Roland Barthes: Structuralism and After*, a comprehensive book on Barthes which develops a linguistic argument based on the Saussurian distinction between *langue* (language) and *parole* (discourse).

And yet, in spite of all the secondhand influence of Saussure through Viggo Bröndal, from whom Barthes took the notion of zero degree, *Writing Degree Zero* is built on a reflection, or a series of reflections, sometimes ambiguous and contradictory, on history. This compromise between historical awareness and formalist fascination is what I call the first paradox of Roland Barthes. It often makes Barthes's argument obscure, while later the *doxa* simplified every problem with the label "structuralism." Nevertheless, not every critic read *Writing Degree Zero* as a structuralist work. Steven Ungar judges that its project is "decidedly historical" and complains, in *Roland Barthes: The Professor of Desire*, about the reaction of critics who associated Barthes's early work with structural linguistics: "The historical project in *Writing Degree Zero* is two-fold: Barthes wants to specify the social and historical nature of writing as an activity whose product is the result of the writer's decision of how to use the language that society prescribes as acceptable for literary purposes . . . In addition, Barthes outlines a study of Literature whose ties with other social institutions he wants to trace historically."[2] The two sparks which produced the book were Barthes's university experience—he studied at the Sorbonne, where literary history and Lansonism reigned supreme,[3] and from 1948 to 1954 held different jobs in education[4]—and existentialism—the articles that constitute *Writing Degree Zero* were first published in *Combat*, a journal Albert Camus edited. It would be too simplistic to think that at this point Barthes had liquidated the university's brand of literary history in order to assume existentialism. As Lavers points out, any new critic beginning to write in the 1950s had to take into consideration the existentialist debate on liberty and the writer's commitment. But this does not mean that Barthes disregarded the questions resulting from the academic world and the institution of literary history.

The most innovative argument of *Writing Degree Zero* lies in the idea of the historicity of literary forms—including language, or, as Lavers has said, the dialectic between *langue* and *parole*. The Sartrean brand of Marxism was thus displaced. Barthes was not concerned with situating works in relation to economic production. He found himself in the position of Walter Benjamin when the latter maintained, in his 1934 article "The Author as Producer," that one has to situate literature in relation to *literary* production: "Rather than ask, 'What is the *attitude* of a work to the relations of production of its time?' I should like to ask, 'What is its *position* in them?' This question directly concerns the function the work has within the literary relations of production of its time. It is concerned, in other words, directly with the literary *technique* of works."[5] Benjamin's concept of technique, which "provides the dialectical starting point from which the unfruitful antithesis of form and content can be surpassed," is not very far from the Barthesian concept of writing, defined as a formal reality: "Within any literary form, there is a general choice of tone, of ethos, if you like, and this is precisely where the writer shows himself clearly as an individual because this is where he commits himself."[6] This concept will subsequently, in 1960, be reformulated as signification, that is, "the union of what signifies and of what is signified: which is to say, again: neither form nor content [the surpassing of the antithesis between form and content, Benjamin would have said], but the proceedings between them."[7] Formal reality, for Barthes, implies relation and not nature. When Barthes wrote *Writing Degree Zero*, he considered an author's style and the language he borrows to be what is natural: his style because it is the writer's very body, mannerisms, and images; his language because it is the code of prescriptions and habits that all writers of a given period have in common. Both formal realities, Barthes's writing and Benjamin's technique, share the quality of *situation*. Benjamin's main example of technique is Brecht's dramatic "laboratory," which stands in opposition to "the total dramatic artwork"[8]: it is an epic theater less concerned with developing actions than with presenting situations, which is to say that it brings into relation two forces of a different nature, as in a chemical experiment. The essence of such theater lies in a choice, and in the author's consciousness of a choice. Barthes's writing is, similarly, a function, a situation, the relation between creation and society, that is to say, between style and language; it therefore becomes literary language as transformed by the writer.

Insisting on this comparison between Barthes and Benjamin does not mean that Barthes read Benjamin, either at the time of *Writing Degree Zero* or later. Barthes actually never speaks of Benjamin, not even in *Camera Lucida*, where he studies the art of photography, although Benjamin's name appears in Barthes's bibliography for his course on the Neuter at the Collège de France in 1978.[9] As he wrote in *Roland Barthes*,[10] his cultural references, in the 1950s, were Sartre, Marx, and Brecht, whom he discovered in 1954, when he started writing in *Théâtre populaire*. My comparison aims to show some implications of *Writing Degree Zero* which go beyond the Sartrean debate. Ungar accurately defines the distinction between Sartre and Barthes as a difference in political hopes: the former wants to mold "wartime solidarity into a peacetime commitment to change society," and the latter realizes "the diminished options of the writer to affect any kind of direct social change."[11] Philippe Roger, in a major chapter of his *Roland Barthes, roman* where he retraces Barthes's relationship with Camus, remarks that *Writing Degree Zero*, far from committing literary form, "shows all the deadlocks of commitment." Roger sees Barthes attracted to "two antagonistic poles, between which no other mediation is possible but a rhetorical one: a 'tragic sense' of writing (and of the world); and on the other hand the intellectual seduction of the principles of 'explanation' which are offered to him by Sartrean analysis and Marxist-oriented sociology."[12] I would say that, in the 1950s, Barthes's political hopes were quite consistent and that, not unlike Benjamin, he believed in the politics of form. He was undoubtedly aware of the contradiction peculiar to modern literature, a tragic disparity between what the writer does and what he sees, between the legacy of literary language and the novelty of the present world. But such a tragic and contradictory condition is a productive one: it creates debates, new attempts, new forms. It carries all the impulses of utopia: the writer knows more and more that language and society cannot be reconciled, but he tries the impossible.

As Ungar points out, Barthes is not a political writer in a strict sense, but he is concerned with political issues. The theme of commitment fascinates him. Only later would he be repelled by all militant language. But at the time of *Writing Degree Zero*, he believed in a commitment through form. Writing implies a choice and a destiny. This means that writing, according to Barthes, is to be found between history—pure, full—and what is not history: language resides completely within history, and style, completely outside it, in the dull materiality of the individual. In short, one does not choose a style, the way one does not choose one's own voice or body: it comes naturally. We cannot choose history, for it is almost entirely outside us and ties us to itself fatally. All the same, there is a moment, belonging to the present, in which we act in history and create the present: this moment depends on individual commitment and requires an existential choice. But once this moment is past, all that we do and write is engulfed by history, or remains completely outside of it, to be lost or forgotten. Thanks to the ephemeral life of writing, Barthes identifies not only the double nature of writing, but also the double nature of history, the mutual and continuous flanking of history and forgetting. This duplicity of history allows for variations within historical studies; it also made possible the history of the *Annales*, in which silences speak and the marginal and forgotten come into focus.

Writing: it is a brief moment, a spark that lasts the tragic time span in which the choice is made, the minute during which the author, facing the white page, decides which compromise to adopt between the freedom of choice and what history presents to him or imposes upon him as literary forms:

> It is not granted to the writer to choose his mode of writing from a kind of non-temporal store of literary forms. It is under the pressure of History and Tradition that the possible modes of writing for a given writer are established; there is a History of Writing. But this History is dual: at the very moment when general History proposes—or imposes—new problematics of the literary language, writing still remains full of the recollection of previous usage, for language is never innocent: words have a second-order memory which mysteriously persists in the midst of new meanings. Writing is precisely this compromise between freedom and remembrance, it is this freedom which remembers and is free only in the gesture of choice, but is no longer so within duration.[13]

One cannot understand the existential implication of freedom, the responsibility borne out of choice, the imprisonment in the ephemeral, if one does not institute a historical type of opposition between traditional and modern. One must mark out the route of an entire period that began with the second half of the nineteenth century and still lasts—or almost. This era witnessed the advent of modernity, and coincided with a great crisis in history, a crisis in the power of reason, in the human power of mastering reality. Barthes calls this crisis a rupture of language and situates its origins between Balzac and Flaubert. The rupture was deeper than any difference between the schools they belonged to: "What contrasts their modes of writing is an essential break, at the precise moment when a new economic structure is joined to an older one, thereby bringing about decisive changes in mentality and consciousness."[14] This proposition is essential because it engages the formalist concept of writing in a resolutely historical context—where one recognizes Marxism and the Marxist concern with the economic structure as determining changes in the superstructure. In spite of the emphasis he placed on the solitude of the writer who chooses his writing all by himself, Barthes was far from proclaiming the solipsistic autonomy of literature and language. He sought instead to read the literary work in history, to assert the historical character of literary forms.

This is the paradox of *Writing Degree Zero*, and it pertains to the title itself, which comes from the linguist Viggo Bröndal: Saussurian influences are obvious but indirect since Barthes only read Saussure later. Barthes strongly emphasized his incipit with a linguistic terminology: "We know that a language is a corpus of prescriptions and habits common to all the writers of a period."[15] But in spite of that, the real problem for Barthes was the relationship between literary form and history. The problem of commitment, derived from the impact of Sartre's *What Is Literature?* was frozen in the neutral mark of the "zero degree," or "white writing"–exemplified by Camus, Kafka, Blanchot, Queneau, and Cayrol. As Susan Sontag remarks in her preface to *Writing Degree Zero*, where she stresses its polemic character within the left-wing literary community, "Barthes is challenging the most intelligent version of the theory of literature's obligation to be socially committed."[16] Ungar recognizes the negative position of Barthes, who, between "Sartre's call to mobilize the writer to social activity and the complete paralysis of radical nihilism,"[17] underlines the alienated condition of the writer, who would demean himself by using the language of our utilitarian society, and is therefore always threatened by silence. But if we give more weight to the academic component of *Writing Degree Zero*, we can see that the real problem for Barthes was to make so-called literary history more historical. This displaces the problem of history inside the discipline of literature, its institution, and does not let it rest only within the consciousness of the writer, who has to decide if he will take a stand in contemporary history or withdraw from history in order to adopt one of the splendid and lifeless languages offered by literary tradition. Addressing the historicity of literary history means to open the debate not only to the world of writers, but to the world of critics and professors of literature: it promotes the role of criticism as the only discipline that can indicate the limits and the necessary utopias of the writers. Literary modernity consists of the interplay between stylistic experiments and critical awareness: it assumes the split between the revolutionary intention of any avant-garde attempt and its falling back into the code of tradition. Such a split is an inevitable condition and one should not try to resolve it. One can only study its occurrences and their depth. One can write the history of the split; this history would be the history of writing Barthes talked about in his introduction, as opposed to the history of literature which is just a peaceful sequence of authors and movements. Therefore, Flaubert is given as a crucial moment in the history of writing, as one of the forerunners of literary modernity, because he understood literature as a technique, and because he is the writer of the split. In 1852, commenting on *Sentimental Education*, he wrote to Louise Colet: "There are in me, literarily speaking, two distinct persons: one who is infatuated with bombast, lyricism, eagle flights, sonorities of phrase and lofty ideas; and another who digs and burrows into the truth as deeply as he can, who likes to treat a humble fact as respectfully as a big one, who would like to make you feel almost *physically* the things he reproduces. The latter likes to laugh, and enjoys the animal side of man."[18]

The project of a history of writing forces one to confront history and rethink its definition, not only in existential terms, but also in disciplinary terms. The question of commitment shifts from the political world to the professional one, with no ambition for an idealistic synthesis between all levels of reality.

Roger speaks of an unbalance in *Writing Degree Zero:* "One finds there a curious collision of heterogeneous languages overlapping without ever fusing."[19] Similarly, Ungar considers *Writing Degree Zero* as being problematic because of the convergence of literature, history, and writing, and because of Barthes's middle position between nihilism and commitment, just before the heroic moment of the structuralist hope, and long before the moment of rejection of any militant attitude, and a Proustian retreat into the world of "les intermittences du coeur," of "circular memories."[20] But, in the early 1950s, Barthes overcame the negativity attached to the alienated condition of the writer by the positive suggestion of new critical openings, new problems, different periodizations. As he declared in an interview with Stephen Heath in 1971, the problem with *Writing Degree Zero* was that he was thinking in terms of traditional history.[21] Nevertheless, hinting at problems of symbolic forms and mentalities, he was forcing all the limits of traditional and nontraditional history: the Hegelian privilege given to political history, the Marxist one given to economic history, the Sartrean one given to the expression of a personal position in contemporary events. Above all, Barthes challenged the institution of literary history.

A Historical Problem

Lansonism, which still represented then the institution of literary history in France, had nothing historical about it, except the name, because it was a series of monographs on authors who were studied in isolation, a succession of lone men, a canon of great writers. In other words, this history was no history at all. It was nothing but a series of chronicles. So at least Barthes said in his article "History or Literature?" published in *Annales* in 1960 and later included in *On Racine*. In the introduction of *Writing Degree Zero*, he had written that literary history imposes what it deems as literature, and makes it a sacred institution: "This hieratic quality of written Signs establishes Literature as an institution and clearly tends to place it above History, for no limits can be set without some idea of permanence. Now it is when history is denied that it is most unmistakably at work."[22] It is, however, absurd that a discipline purporting to be historical ends up by excluding history. Barthes, on the other hand, proposed a confrontation between history and literature. Above all, he wanted to put an end to the sacredness of the literary institution: the only gesture that can desecrate or break the instituted ritual, necessarily tied to the past, consists in reckoning with the present, in studying journalism or literary techniques, as Benjamin did, or in distinguishing the varieties of French writing, as Barthes does: "The unity of classical writing, which remained uniform for centuries, the plurality of its modes in modern times, increased in the last hundred years until it came near to questioning the very fact of literature, this kind of disintegration of French writing does indeed correspond to a great crisis in general History, which is noticeable in literary History proper, only much more confusedly."[23]

Moreover, Barthes wanted to liberate literature from

those isolated series of authors, from the linear succession of monographs, because history is not a sequence but a constellation of forces, a process placing things in relation to each other and, one might also say, the point of contact between structure and event, between generality and particularity.

One should not let oneself be trapped by terminology: in the end, the division in *Writing Degree Zero* between *langue* and *parole*—like the division between language, style, and writing—is of little importance. Barthes is not concerned with precise, impeccable definitions. We will see later how Barthes thrived on ambiguity, on allusions rich in ideas. What really counts is to speak with another vocabulary, or to enrich one's vocabulary in order to find other solutions and to formulate other questions. It is almost a trick, an artifice: Barthes adds to Sartre's binary opposition between language and style the term of writing. It therefore becomes possible to trace a history of literary language "which is neither that of a particular language, nor that of the various styles, but simply that of the Signs of Literature, and we can expect that this purely formal history may manifest, in its far from obscure way, a link with the deeper levels of History."[24]

Academic literary history is insufficient because of its isolationist nature, and the Sartrean approach suffocates the specificity of literature, because it does not manage to grasp its formal character and remains impeded by old distinctions, such as prose and poetry.[25] Barthes tried to find terms that would free literature from an eternal oscillation between political realism and art for art's sake, between commitment and the aestheticizing cult of good writing. Barthes stopped asking the question "Why write?" in order to ask "How can we write, today?" In this manner, he remained suspended between a tone characteristic of the political avant-garde, and another tone, that of the historian. For example, in a single paragraph he stigmatized an entire literary evolution, the one that founded modernity:

The whole nineteenth century witnessed the progress of this dramatic phenomenon of concretion. In Chateaubriand it is still only a trace, a light pressure of linguistic euphoria, a kind of narcissism in which the manner of writing is scarcely separable from its instrumental function and merely mirrors itself. Flaubert—to take only the typical stages of this process—finally established Literature as an object, through promoting literary labor to the status of a value; form became the end-product of craftsmanship, like a piece of pottery or a jewel (one must understand that craftsmanship was here made manifest, that is, it was for the first time imposed to the reader as a spectacle). Mallarmé's work, finally, was the crowning achievement of this creation of Literature as Object, and this by the ultimate of all objectifying acts: murder. For we know that the whole effort of Mallarmé was exerted towards the destruction of language, with Literature reduced, so to speak, to become its carcass.[26]

The style of literary history—listing names of authors, dating events, dividing into periods, describing the progression of a literary phenomenon—is overwhelmed by the sweep of history, the need to generalize, to speak at once of a whole century. The overall tone does violence to the positivist grayness imposed by Lanson, who wanted to make truth, and not beauty, speak, and who was in favor of giving up style.[27] There arises in this passage of *Writing Degree Zero* a kind of colorism, which is part aesthetic, part dramatic, as well as mythical and allegorical. Allegory is meant here in the rhetorical sense, which gives each proposition a double meaning, one literal and the other spiritual, and presents a thought—in this case the objectification of literature—by using the image of another thought—ceramics, a jewel, a carcass. Just as Michel Foucault, in *Madness and Civilization*, was to show personified leprosy leaving the town walls of the Renaissance city,[28] here Barthes originates, still in the Sartrean vein, a style, or a writing—it matters little—that catches the eye with the sparkle of a jewel, the violence of a crime, or the apparition of a cadaver: in short, it offers the real spectacle of modern literature taking on symbolic value in a genre that results from the contamination of classical allegory, founded on a very transparent double sense,[29] by realistic description, such as it existed in the nineteenth-century novel.

There are innumerable examples of such a style in *Writing Degree Zero:* they bear witness to a gesture of revolt against the repressiveness of the style dictated by Lansonism, as though Barthes wished to deny the law that prohibits the critic from dancing with his pen. In this anti-Lansonism is to be found the meaning of the idea that was most constant in Barthes's intellectual life through all his transformations, namely, that the fusion between criticism and literature is the most fundamental fact of literary modernity, and that after Mallarmé there came about a real and true unification of the poetic and critical function of writing, as in Proust, Joyce, Musil, etc.

As for the avant-garde tone, one must realize that, in stylistic terms, it partakes of the allegorical tendency already mentioned:

> There is therefore in every present mode of writing a double postulation: there is the impetus of a break and the impetus of a coming to power, there is the very shape of every revolutionary situation, the fundamental ambiguity of which is that Revolution must of necessity borrow, from what it wants to destroy, the very image of what it wants to possess. Like modern art in its entirety, literary writing carries at the same time the alienation of History and the dream of History; as a Necessity, it testifies to the division of languages which is inseparable from the division of classes; as Freedom, it is the consciousness of this division and the very effort which seeks to surmount it.[30]

This passage illustrates well Barthes's attitude toward the artistic avant-garde: no myths of liberation, but, instead, what almost amounts to a denunciation of avant-garde myths. The writer is inevitably in an ambiguous position because, as Benjamin would say, the revolutionary intellectual has received culture as a dowry from the bourgeois class. Barthes could not believe in the uniformity of the revolutionary attitude, or in the eternity of a form of writing. The individual who writes is torn by guilt when he confronts the revolution. This guilt is provoked by the solitude of his own enterprise. If one were to give up this solitude, one would end up by writing militant literature, one would fall, literally, into propaganda: "Any political mode of writing can only uphold a police world."[31] The writer is also guilty because he wants to write well: the solitude of writing is accompanied by an "imagination eagerly desiring a felicity,"[32] which seeks a dream language, fresh and capable of prefiguring an idyllic world in which language would no longer be alienated. This is the dilemma of the leftist writer, who, like Marx himself, is convinced that linguistic signs, like all signs, are alienated, and who literarily and politically desires the great utopia of nonalienated language. Such a utopia represents the very conflict of the modern writer in the face of the avant-garde destiny: the form which artistically appears to be a point of rupture or a moment of newness is destined to be reproduced, to become automatic.

Thus the writing of Breton and Gide became tradition: unfortunately, no language can keep the freshness of its initial explosion. It becomes used, coded, instituted: we can see here a hint of the argument against language, which I will develop in the second chapter. After 1820, after the solidity of the classical code had crumbled, making room for the multiplicity of modern writing, the writer was forced to take on the labor of Sisyphus and continually seek originality. Since World War II, he has had to reckon with intellectual and existential commitment as well. Sartrean and anti-Sartrean at once, *Writing Degree Zero* is a book in which Barthes wants to put an end to the postwar thematic of commitment. He also signals the major contemporary writings, like Blanchot's and Bataille's works, which were appearing outside the debate on the correct political positions. Barthes behaved therefore like a literary critic writing in magazines and updating the taste for new literature. His work is made of that journalistic technique Benjamin had seen as the new literary form of the twentieth century.

What emerges from *Writing Degree Zero* is the desire to write, to write well, and to reach a morality of the form instead of falling into aestheticism. True, language is alienated, and every work of art is part of a cycle of economic production: it is naive to believe that one could escape the cycle and experience pure artistic creation, that one could enjoy a utopian harmony between the artistic and the productive spheres. All this is true. But today it is useless to consider these questions and their common answers. These ideas may be dated; they reflect the anguish that followed the war, which can be called the tyranny of practice or the desperate attempt to make practice and theory coincide. Roger analyzes the changes from the *Combat* article, "Le Sentiment tragique de l'écriture" (14 December 1950), to the article concluding *Writing Degree Zero*, "The Utopia of Language." What was called tragedy in *Combat* becomes utopia, while the nostalgia for the *écriture littéraire*, which was "more and more a magnificent and deserted sign" and appeared as threatened by "a literature of explanation and struggle,"[33] is transfigured into the promise of new forms. It is as if the fascination for the theme of commitment forced Barthes to feel positive about the tragedy of writing. Facing the reactionary illusions of literary writing, beautiful style, pleasure in culture and art, and at the same time the leftist illusion of the reconciliation of the political and the artistic, Barthes did not want to be trapped in either position. He wanted to be a leftist without the leftist illusion, and he wanted to love literature passionately without being reactionary. Later on, in 1975, when he was tired of the stereotypes of political discourse, he imagined Brecht criticizing him, since he was not ready to "be sacrificed to politics,"[34] and he remarked that his place was language. His place had always been language. Roger reminds us that Maurice Nadeau introduced Barthes to the readers of *Combat*, in 1947, as a fanatic of language, "un enragé du langage."[35] Nevertheless, rage bears the energy to fight. *Writing Degree Zero* says that the only solution for one who writes is to assume the responsibility of form, the professionalism of writing, the quest for a style. Barthes knows the tragedy of the writer, but he is not yet overwhelmed by the fatigue with stereotypes—political, structuralist, psychoanalytical, etc. His attraction to the idea itself of tragedy comes also from his classical studies at the university, as shown by his first article, "Culture et tragédie"[36]: what could be more exalting for a young critic than finding a link between the old culture coming from the university and real life, between past and present? Myth is not a bookish notion, it is a real force, behind many human behaviors. One feels a strong intellectual excitement when academic knowledge embraces something that overcomes the pure academic world and reaches life.

A utopia, the utopia of language in *Writing Degree Zero*, is at once a force, a tendency, a productive negativity. But nothing of the kind exists, just as that absolutely neutral writing, of which the best examples for Barthes would be the recent works of Camus and Blanchot, is nowhere a reality. The reason is always the same: barely has a form been realized when it becomes an institution. The historical drama that made it possible, the very history that created it, congeals and hardens it so that it is turned on some level into a stereotype. One could say the same thing about political power and the alternation of power. Barthes demonstrates here all the ambiguity of leftist thinking, in art as in politics: it is simultaneously a struggle against institutions and traditions and the will to become part of those institutions and traditions. And Barthes reveals his basic anarchic nature, in the style of Camus rather than Sartre. This point is essential not only in order to understand *Writing Degree Zero* but also because it constitutes the very essence of Barthesian thought, even in his last works. It constitutes the essence of his style as a critic, the very core of his eclecticism, making pluralism a moral and intellectual necessity with regard to form. Later we will examine the anarchic developments of such a conception. But the term "development" is misleading; one should say the obsessive knots, in short, all that constitutes the deep individuality of an author, his body and mannerisms, which in *Writing Degree Zero* are defined as the style of a writer.

Even though *Writing Degree Zero* ends with a chapter on the utopia of language, and announces new forms of literature, its basic tone is tragic, pessimistic, not only because responsibility is inescapable, but also because the conflict between the individual and society is insurmountable.[37] Modern literature is the most privileged and painful place for such a conflict; it is constitutionally alienated and divided, rendered permanently impotent. But, paradoxically, the writer continues to write and to want to write in spite of his impotence, enraged with language: a gesture of lucid folly, an inevitable act of loss, similar to Orpheus's turning backward. The paradox of Barthes in *Writing Degree Zero* corresponds to an oscillation between despair and energy.

The ideal and radical continuation of *Writing Degree Zero* is not the Barthes of the 1960s, the semiologist carried away by the hope for a new method that would make literature scientific and provide intellectuals with precise tools for social analysis; the continuation of *Writing Degree Zero* is the obsessive image of Orpheus's backward glance and of the solitude of the act of writing, an image found in Blanchot's *The Space of Literature*, published in 1955 and based on older articles from *La Nouvelle Revue française*. Considering the influence of Blanchot on Barthes, we can also say that Barthes's first book is the continuation of "The Essential Solitude," the first part of *The Space of Literature*. Artistic creativity, Blanchot maintained, quoting Hölderlin, reveals itself as insufficient to the one who has chosen it "at the decisive hour—those hours that ring every hour—when 'the poet must complete his message by renouncing himself.' "[38]

One must place in this pessimism, which has recently been confused with nihilism by Tzvetan Todorov, in its historical context.[39] One must understand how this consciousness of the artistic act is the only one that could both block the illusion of the avant-garde and permit the continuation of literature, simply by declaring its death: Mallarmé's crime, Blanchot's *écriture blanche*, "white writing." In an intellectual environment influenced by the surrealist epic, by Gide, Aragon, by the committed tone of *Les Temps modernes*, this negative thinking about literature was more than beneficial.

The style of *Writing Degree Zero*—as we have already seen—approaches and thwarts critical language; it remains completely general in that no particular author or work is analyzed, but, on the other hand, it is not purely theoretical or methodological, and does not rely on philosophy for its justification. Instead it takes the form of critical *poèmes en prose*, of critical illuminations in which the aphorism is extremely figured and is continued by a necessary explanation that is never simply didactic. Born at the sign of the author's lacerating ambiguity, *Writing Degree Zero* splinters into brief essays, but its fragmentation is balanced by the schematism of its definitions—language, style, writing—and the poetic, evocative style—for example, the secret of style is "recollection locked within the body of the writer."[40] Blanchot wrote in his review: "A recent essay by Roland Barthes, one of those rare books in which the future of literature is inscribed."[41]

The Limit of History: Silence

The future of literature is not to be found in an ideology, but it can be founded in a style, on the strength of an idea.

Style is defined by Barthes as the body of the writer, and the idea of *Writing Degree Zero* is the physiology of the modern in literature, from a point of view where language is seen as the cultural horizon of the twentieth century. One could say that this book articulated, *ante literam*, those very conditions which today we call postmodern: frenetic pluralism, the encounter between the excessively historical and what has been extrapolated from history while remaining marked by the absence of historicity and the lack of affiliation with any school. One must consequently understand the modern as what is given rather than what is hoped for, as impotence rather than the advent of the new, as anguish and the assumption of anguish, as the metropolitan condition perceived by Baudelaire and Benjamin—a condition from which one cannot return to a harmonious community because it has internalized the violence of the great city.[42]

In *The Space of Literature*, Blanchot talks about the Austrian writer Hugo von Hofmannsthal, of his temptation to stop writing and be silent, which is so clear in *The Letter of Lord Chandos* (1901). Chandos concludes his letter to his friend Francis Bacon with these decisive words: "I felt, with a certainty not entirely bereft of a feeling of sorrow, that neither in the coming year nor in the following nor in all the years of this my life shall I write a book, whether in English or in Latin."[43] Barthes winds up not far from the position of Hofmannsthal when Chandos says that he sees words in front of him as though they were eyes staring at him: "Single words floated round me; they congealed into eyes which stared at me and into which I was forced to stare back—whirlpools which gave me vertigo and, reeling incessantly, led into the void."[44] The rapprochement with the Austrian writer can offer another insight into the understanding of literary modernity as crisis, alienation, silence, and endless nostalgia for the "splendid and deserted" world of literature. Isolated words, words as things: thick, consistent, heavy as matter. Such is the form-object or the literature-object evoked in *Writing Degree Zero*, which re-echoes the word treated as a thing, as an object in poetry, which Sartre speaks of in *What Is Literature?* when he describes the poet as a man who sees words as natural things, like grass or trees.[45] Such is the word in modern poetry, as discussed by Barthes in the chapter "Is There Any Poetic Writing?" which rises straight, dense, and consistent "like a monolith, or a pillar . . . it is a sign which stands . . . an act without immediate past, without environment"; the poetic word is a "dwelling place."[46] The chapter "Writing and Silence" indicates the zero degree, the neutral point of writing with Mallarmé and Blanchot. They both take the position of silence, as Lord Chandos does in his letter to Francis Bacon when he explains why he can no longer write or study literary works conceived in times that had faith in the classical code, that saw language as the expression of the harmonious relation between a being and the world. Faced with the decay and the crumbling of the classical order, Chandos chooses silence. To be silent, or almost, such was Mallarmé's choice, according to Barthes:

> Mallarmé's typographical agraphia seeks to create around rarefied words an empty zone . . . This art has the very structure of suicide: in it, silence is an homogeneous poetic time which traps the word between two layers and sets it off less as a fragment of a cryptogram than as a light, a void, a murder, a freedom. (We know all that this hypothesis of Mallarmé as a murderer of language owes to Blanchot.) This language of Mallarmé's is like Orpheus who can save what he loves only by renouncing it, and who, just the same, cannot resist glancing round a little; it is Literature brought to the gates of the Promised Land: a world without Literature, but one to which writers would nevertheless have to bear witness.[47]

Barthes never mentions Hofmannsthal, even though he speaks in *Writing Degree Zero*, as well as in *Critical Essays*, of Kafka as a writer who reached the rarefied and reified language of the modern. Benjamin saw Kafka in the same way, while Hofmannsthal, in his opinion, betrayed the language of the modern which he had perceived and understood at the time of *The Letter of Lord Chandos*. He wrote to Adorno: "Julian [in Hofmannsthal's *The Tower*] betrays the Prince: Hofmannsthal turned away from the task he indicated in *The Letter of Lord Chandos*. His silence was a sort of punishment. The language that concealed from Hofmannsthal could actually be the one that, in the same years, was given to Kafka, because Kafka took on himself the task which Hofmannsthal renounced morally and therefore poetically."[48] We could similarly say that the early Barthes reached the modern when he dealt with contemporary literature, in *Writing Degree Zero* and in his articles on Robbe-Grillet and the *Nouveau Roman;* nevertheless he always flirted with the classics, the nineteenth-century classics, like Balzac. He openly declared in *Roland Barthes* that he wrote *classique*,[49] and he admitted in 1977, at the time Proust became more and more the writer whom he spoke of, that "all of a sudden, it has become a matter of indifference to me whether or not I'm modern."[50] Should we think that, not unlike Hofmannsthal, he betrayed the modern and became revisionist, if not reactionary? Or should we read in his intellectual adventure, in the many transformations and constant leitmotif of his work, the old ambivalence of art, between the ephemeral and the eternal, to use Baudelaire's terms? Probably the paradox which contains all Barthes's paradoxes, the paradox which my whole reading of Barthes aims at, is the one expressed or, better, dictated by the poet of the modern: "In a word, for any *modernity* to deserve becoming ancient, one should have extracted from it the mysterious beauty involuntarily infused by human life."[51]

Blanchot speaks of *The Letter of Lord Chandos* in the chapter on inspiration of *The Space of Literature*, where he understands silence as an element constituting the writer's daily practice, the moment when inspiration and the lack of inspiration fuse: an arid, sterile moment of suspension, a standstill. This corresponds well to Hofmannsthal's biography, where a moment of crisis put an end to his poetic production under the name Loris and forced him to suspend the pleasure of his sensualist and ornate language. But Barthes is somewhat closer to Hofmannsthal's transfiguration of his personal crisis into a historical one. Silence is an individual condition deriving from a historical condition, be it Lord Chandos's and Francis Bacon's England at the beginning of the seventeenth century, Austria at the beginning of the nineteenth century, or France after World War II. The writer's daily practice is subject to the cruel law of his time: modernity is the broken dream, Orpheus incessantly turning back to kill what he loves. If we consider the modalities of zero degree, we can push the parallel with Hofmannsthal even further. On the one hand, there is a mode of writing which is all light, crime, and violence, of the Mallarmé type; on the other, there is the completely journalistic writing—a pure journalism, devoid of all pathos—of Camus, a style without style, which voluntarily gave up all elegance and ornamentation, factors that take writing back in time and drape it in history. This neutrality, which is not opacity but metallic gleam, this absolute nudity is similar to the cruel geometry of Kafka's language. It is the nudity of tragedy, of art, "which only art can attain," wrote Barthes in his first published article, "Culture et tragédie."[52] Nudity represents the artistic ideal expressed by Hofmannsthal in his article of 1903, "The Stage as Dream Image," in which the stage designer is seen as someone who gives up ornamentation: "He should have great power to dream, and he should be a poet among poets. His eye should be like the eye of the dreamer . . . The economy of dreams is indescribable. Who can forget how in dreams there prevails a great violence accompanied by simplicity, by marvelous spareness?"[53]

The stage designer must be a poet among poets. He must have the characteristic of the poet as Hofmannsthal describes him in "The Poet and His Time," an essay Blanchot found striking.[54] The poet is a relentless spectator who cannot neglect anything. His eyes should have no lids and always be looking, in the same kind of obsessed stare that Lord Chandos had when he saw words as though they were actual objects and the words seemed like eyes staring at him. Hofmannsthal's poet must know how to register all the movements of his era like a seismograph; he should be an author of novels, a journalist, a common man, the impersonal presence behind all things, the voice of the night and of silence. For Hofmannsthal, as for Barthes and Blanchot, the contemporary poet—or writer—is in the end thoroughly a creature of his times, impregnated by the present and, paradoxically, one who renounces history by rejecting ornamentation, the very delight of his era, as the seductions of history. The modern writer is one who moves in the atemporality and ahistoricity of the dream—or of tragedy, according to Barthes's first article on tragedy, whose sense is not in time, but "in an immediate universe stripped of the very gates of Time."[55] (In *Roland Barthes*, Barthes found Fourier more important historically than Flaubert, even if in Fourier's work "there is virtually no direct trace" of his contemporary history, whereas "Flaubert narrates in the course of a novel all the events of 1948." But "Fourier has indirectly expressed the desire of History."[56]) The vertigo of the modern man, as Nietzsche and Bataille felt, crystallizes around the idea that we are at the end of history.

Just as it would be a mistake to read *Writing Degree Zero* as though it were completely and exclusively immersed in the Sartrean *doxa*, so it would also be a mistake to see Barthes in a total mystic attitude. Such a vision would lead one too easily to deduce a homology between Barthes and Blanchot.[57] I do not mean to draw a strong contrast between Barthes and Blanchot, who definitively share what can be called the religion of literature, but I would like to indicate their differences in temperament—in the way Baudelaire spoke of temperament for painters. In intellectual or literary terms they belong to the same movement, the contemporary swan's song of literature. But in terms of style—that style which is the body of the writer—Blanchot has the temperament of the mystical, Barthes, of the realist. We could even reinstate a difference between prose and poetry: unlike Blanchot, who is so attracted to German poets, Barthes does not work with poets; his favorite ground is the nineteenth-century French novel. We will deal in the next two chapters with the question of reality and realism for Barthes, and with his search for a prose genre close to the traditional novel or the critical essay—or a mixture of the two. Barthes insists that the zero degree or white writing, even though it manages to express the emptiness of modern man and indicate the end of literature, ends by becoming a stereotype, a cliché. He thereby blocks the very absolutism of silence, breaking its beautiful and cruel myth, its negative compliance. Discreetly, without any emphasis, Barthes upholds an affirmative value in *Writing Degree Zero*, even though, as I have said, the basic tone is tragic: the affirmative value I am referring to is the will. Writing is an act of will, which must be all the stronger if one is disenchanted. Moreover, the fact that literature has become a language problem opens up new horizons, "a new humanism," Barthes says, in which, perhaps, there will be "a reconciliation between the logos of the writer and that of men."[58] French literature, having abandoned the high classical code since the advent of bourgeois writing around 1830, multiplied itself in the attempt to reproduce the many languages spoken and lived by men, so that in Proust an individual's entire being is identified with his language.

The will to write is a form of work: work emerges as the background and foundation of all of *Writing Degree Zero*, and not just because, around 1850,

> a whole class of writers anxious to assume to the full the responsibility of their tradition is about to put the work-value of writing in place of its usage-value. Writing is now to be saved not by virtue of what it exists

History
and
Form

24

for, but thanks to the work it has cost. There begins now to grow up an image of the writer as a craftsman who shuts himself away in some legendary place, like a workman operating at home, and who roughs out, cuts, polishes and sets his form exactly as a jeweler extracts art from his material, devoting to his work regular hours of solitary effort.[59]

Work is also seen as desire, the labor of Sisyphus and the professional technique of the writer. In fact, I would say that the will to write, the anguish, the sense of guilt and utopia, in short, the whole ambiguity of the modern writer, represent a real and typical phenomenology of work in which objective and subjective facts are fused and confused in a unity overcoming the dichotomy between the individual and society. Later, Barthes will end *Roland Barthes* with a fragment entitled "The Monster of Totality": "Different discourse: this August 6, the countryside, the morning of a splendid day: sun, warmth, flowers, silence, calm, radiance. Nothing stirs, neither desire nor aggression; only the task is there, the work before me, like a kind of universal being: everything is full. Then that would be Nature? An absence . . . of the rest? Totality?"[60]

Michelet

Work as will, totality, and—there is no other word for it— passion, is not described in *Writing Degree Zero* but emanates from it like a shadow. Even if Orpheus is the image Barthes most often uses to describe the difficulties of writing, the myth that really captures the writer's anguish is the myth of Sisyphus—in the Camus version of it, published in 1942: the divorce between a man and his life, the sense of the absurd.[61] The brutality, repetitiveness, and uselessness of the work—what's the point of writing?—is a sentence imposed not by others, but by the writer himself. But what if this work, once negative, chilling, and white, once crystalline and metallic, silent and disenchanted, becomes the medium for emphasis, excess, color, fury, and voice? In opposition to the modern writer, who is either faceless and anonymous or has a thousand faces and names, the multiple, pluralistic writings of modernity, in opposition to the French intellectual of the 1950s, who either had Camus's dryness, Sartre's severity, or Blanchot's rarefaction, there arose, from the past, from history, from the beginning of time, embalmed by history and France, the figure of Michelet.

> In the very periods he believed himself threatened by every possible dispersion of the body—i.e., throughout his whole life—this man was possessed by an insensate rage to work. Schedules (draconian), results (vast output), even egoism (which leads him to forsake his first wife and abandon his dying son)—all testify to the fact. Yet this frenzied labor (of inquiry, of erudition, and of writing), governed by a virtually monastic discipline, inveterately sustained its prophetic tension. Routinized in form, it was maintained at a constant tragic pitch.[62]

Michelet becomes the alter ego of the modern writer described in *Writing Degree Zero*, of the poet of the present, whose eyes have no lids: he is simultaneously the modern writer's double and other, both his twin and an alien being. Michelet's history contrasts with the ambiguous history of *Writing Degree Zero*, oscillating between an excess of history and the extreme limit of historicity—that is to say the absence of history. It is simultaneously plant-history, like the history of Herder, and spiral history, like the history of Vico, and it favors above all death, and decadence. The crucial historical periods for Michelet were the final phases of the Roman Empire, the beginning of Christianity, and the Middle Ages; death implied for him the resurrection of history and its very definition, and history was for him the resurrection of the dead.

Michelet, then: one must understand writing as a chemistry, an alchemy, and not as a kind of Hegelian progression. One writes with two hands, and not with one, as though one were playing the piano, in order to dance with one's pen, to follow the dance of history, excessive and Dionysian like a witch's Sabbat. If writing is a technique, then it is also a chemical operation in which elements are mixed together. Writing is the giving of form to formless matter. If the essence of modernity is pluralism, vertigo, the disaggregation of forms, the characteristic of writing is its ephemeral nature, its very liberty which frees it from the body—the style of the writer—until it reaches the fragile line beyond which it will be engulfed by time—history, language, tradition, the automatism of a school. *Writing Degree Zero*, Barthes's first book, was not to be followed by the discovery of semiology, as though such a development were dictated by the simple fact that the notion of zero degree comes from linguistics. *Writing Degree Zero* was written in the same years Barthes published his article "Michelet, l'histoire et la mort" in the review *Esprit* (1951) and his book *Michelet* (1954). If one hand wrote on the tragedy of modernity, the other wrote on the historian of the French Revolution. Barthes's study of Michelet is composed of elements analogous to those found in *Writing Degree Zero*—history, the body, style—but also of elements completely absent from white writing: colors.

One should read *Writing Degree Zero* alongside *Michelet*, just as one should read Hofmannsthal's *The Letter of Lord Chandos* alongside *Letters of a Man Who Returned (Die Briefe des Zurückgekerten)*, written around the same time, instead of isolating it in silence, in the refusal or suspicion of language or in the irremediable split of the self. Rereading *Chandos* alongside *Letters of a Man Who Returned* would give a response, admittedly of a technical and not metaphysical kind, to the anguish of modernity. *Letters of a Man Who Returned* expresses a situation very similar to that of *Chandos* because the first-person narrator, back in Austria and Germany after an absence of many years, is struck by the decadence of Europe and feels he has lost his sense of reality. Objects seem isolated and separate from the continuity of the real, as menacing and alien as the words Chandos saw staring at him like eyes. In the highest moment of anguish, when the most banal gesture has become impossible, right before going to a business meeting which will be decisive for his company, the traveler steps into a gallery where a few paintings are hanging. At that moment the violence of these colors resembles the violence of a visual experience in *Chandos*. While riding his horse, Chandos is suddenly struck by a very vivid scene, which he does not see directly but just imagines: poisoned rats dying in his cellar. He sees them as if they were dying in front of his eyes and feels their terror. In a similar way the paintings are, for the traveler, an intense physical and spiritual experience. The force of their lacerating colorism, which surpasses all impressionism, strikes him as both the objective, real correspondence to his anguish and the very answer to that anguish. He is overcome by a sense of force and takes on a duality of personality which permits him to bring the business meeting to a successful conclusion: "I could feel, could know, could fathom, could enjoy abyss and summit, without and within, one and all in a ten-thousandth part of the time I take to write these words— and was as though two men, but was master over my life, master over my strength, my intellect . . ."[63] The paintings the traveler admired were by Van Gogh—and Van Gogh resembles Michelet in that he could not stop working: "Van Gogh says he cannot stop working," writes Blanchot, apropos the inexhaustibility of inspiration.[64] Van Gogh's extreme violence comes to constitute the language that Chandos could not find. It is the other side of silence, as it is the mute history of the past to which Michelet gives voice, and body:

> Colour. Colour. To me now that sounds a wretched word . . . But truly in no moment am I more a human

being than when I feel myself living with hundred-fold strength, and this happens to me when that which has always lain mute and closed before me and is nothing but massiveness and strangeness, when this opens and, as in a wave of love, entwines me with itself. And am I not then at the inner core of things as much as a human being, as much as myself, as ever I could be— nameless alone; not however petrified in aloneness, but as if there flowed from me in waves the strength that makes me the chosen mate of those strong, silent powers which sit around me mutely as on thrones?[65]

The way out is always to be found in alterity, in excess, and in becoming. To isolate oneself in a typically modern way, like Chandos's silence, or white writing, though it may be fitting, would constitute an eternization, a fixation which borders on mysticism, which in any case is condemned to repetition. Thus, we are today a little weary of the negativity of modern thought, of the split of the *cogito* and the idea of crisis. Perhaps, as Hofmannsthal's traveler and Michelet's work suggest, one can take on this condition, consider it a given fact, and stop describing it. Perhaps one can both know the disintegration of the self and remain in control—not of one's own life, certainly, but of a knowledge, a technique, a *techné*, an art, as Van Gogh did, beyond the myth of torment and madness, or Hofmannsthal's traveler who finally succeeds in his financial dealings. All of which brings us back to the etymological value of *poiein* —to make—and of poetry and art as fabrication of an object.

Writing Degree Zero and *Michelet* form, therefore, a whole, the way *The Letter of Lord Chandos* and *Letters of a Man Who Returned* do. They balance each other out, the way white and the most violent colors do, the way silence and speech do. Each is the continuation of the other, and *Michelet* confirms the thesis of *Writing Degree Zero*, through the analysis of a writing practice completely different from the neutral, geometrical, and white one. Ungar says that *Michelet* "extends the project" announced in Barthes's first book: "It studies the convergence of literary and historical inquiries by an approach to history as discourse and writing."[66] I would say that the link between the two books is less an argument than a stylistic temptation: trying out the difference, knowing that beauty can be both in Ingres's draftsmanship and in Delacroix's colorism. In the Salon of literature and history, the eye can quickly move from one style to another, enjoy variety and contrasts: as Baudelaire said, it is a limited and stubborn vision that insists on just one form of beauty.

Color and the Matter of History

The other writing that Barthes confronts in *Michelet* is first of all the otherness of Michelet. Anyone who both shares some of the avant-garde's values and enjoys Michelet needs courage to rediscover him. Nothing could be less timely than that writer's romanticism, than his emphatic language and the scientific imprecision of his historiography. As Barthes said in a 1974 article, "Michelet is not in fashion. Michelet is not modern."[67] His ideology, which permeates all his work and words, makes him unlikable and impossible for the modern reader: it is plain petit-bourgeois ideology which he never disguises. This petit-bourgeois ideology "is one of those which are not forgiven today, for it is still broadly our own, that of our institutions, of our schools; hence it cannot be taken unseasonably, as can the 'progressive' ideology of the eighteenth-century bourgeoisie."[68]

So why should one read Michelet? Barthes explained why in the 1970s, during a period of renewed interest in Michelet, when his *Correspondence* was published, his historical works were reprinted, an issue of *L'Arc* was devoted to him. Because Michelet, in spite of his ideology, is modern for three reasons. First of all, Barthes explains, as a few historians—Lucien Febvre in particular—have understood, he suggested a new kind of history, which would study the goings-on of daily life, the ways in which people dress, marry, die, and believe in various symbolic representations. Furthermore, Michelet should be readable for all those practicing the new science that Barthes defines as the science of substitution or symbolic equivalence—*Entstellungswissenschaft*—which includes Freudianism, structuralism, and Marxism as well. The third, deepest, and most incomprehensible reason Michelet is modern is that he is a man of *parti-pris*, a man unashamed of his bias. Every one of his discourses was born of a choice, every fact is linked to a meaning, to what Michelet decides to be its meaning. Such an approach is scandalous from a scientific point of view: fact and sense coincide, facts have first a linguistic existence. In this respect Michelet resembles Nietzsche, as Barthes argues in his 1972 article in *L'Arc*, "Michelet, Today."[69] The comparison between Nietzsche and Michelet is particularly striking, since Nietzsche disliked the French historian: "Michelet, enthusiasm in shirtsleeves,"[70] he said in a phrase which captures the populist, petit-bourgeois ideology of the French historian, his focusing on the good things in life. Nietzsche, rightfully an idol of modernity, has provoked readings of every kind which overcome the intolerable appearance of some of his statements from the viewpoint of our democratic culture; these readings are, therefore, capable of surpassing ideology—Nietzsche also had one: that of the decadence and *fin-de-siècle*—and privileging a style, a mode of writing: the aphorism. Why can we not do the same with Michelet? Why can we not consider, for example, how Michelet's writing—the famous lyrical style of his books, of his monumental works—actually was a combination of the organic and the fragmentary, of the continuous and the discontinuous? Barthes remarked how the historian's text is filled with breaks, leaks, holes. One might say, to use Baudelaire's terms, that it is at once concentrated and volatile, or that it is both aphoristic and verbose, giving rise to a sentence both cutting and diluted.

In short, if we develop Barthes's suggestion, we can find in Michelet, if we look beyond his ideology, an absolutely modern dimension, a double constitution or a plurality and promiscuity of languages of an almost expressionistic violence. It is as though the lines of discourse went in all directions, working, like Van Gogh's brush strokes, to overturn the rational rules of perspective.[71]

In *Michelet*, Barthes organizes his reading according to substance, subject, and consistency, as though he had to formulate a treatise on colors that would be capable of explaining their pictorial rather than decorative use and the inexplicable transformation they undergo on passing from the artist's palette to his canvas. The chain of substances identified by Barthes includes what he calls itinerant material, water, water-as-fish, narcotics, blood, stone, dry death, death-as-sleep and death-as-sun, or world-as-woman. It has often been said that Victor Hugo's style is analogous to Delacroix's painting—an idea Baudelaire found disturbing. One ought rather associate Michelet and Delacroix, their use of livid color, their dramatic groupings, their refusal to distinguish details in a proportioned sketch, the emotional tone, their way of capturing figures in motion.

In contrast to *Writing Degree Zero*, which moves between generality and abstraction, which mentions various authors without ever quoting any, *Michelet* presents an author and a text; it is an anthology which collects passages and citations. It tries to rediscover the most concrete thing that can be, the structure of an existence: "That has been my endeavor: to recover the structure of an existence (if not a life), a thematic, if you like, or better still: an organized network of obsessions."[72] But to use the terms of *Writing Degree Zero*, what is this thematic, this nucleus of obsessions, if not what constitutes the author's style? Style, Barthes said in that book, is almost beyond literature, it is life, biology: "Imagery, delivery, vocabulary spring from the body and the past of the writer and gradually become the very reflexes of his art . . . style has always something crude about it . . . Its frame of reference is biological or biographical, not historical: it is the writer's 'thing,' his glory and his prison, it is his solitude."[73] Michelet is therefore a character or a writer who emerges through the violence of his body, his headaches, nausea, toothaches: a real and true coincidence between body and style. His broken body, sensitive to the force of a storm, to cold, "this disjointed physiology seems accessible only to the most brutal constraint of all: work."[74] The elements which in *Writing Degree Zero* remained abstract and disconnected become in *Michelet* concrete and coherent, unified in a single person, a single writer, as though body, work, and Michelet formed a single entity. Michelet's history is nothing other than his way of writing it, his deep biography. It passes through the deaths of history and the deaths of eras, states, empires, and institutions, as though the body of history were always suffering, dying, and constantly being reborn, like Michelet himself, who, at the age of forty-four, thinks he is entering that long torment, old age, but at fifty happily begins a new life with his third wife, who is only twenty-two.

In *Michelet*, history and the body, which stood in opposition in *Writing Degree Zero*, make a whole which integrates writing as well. One sees here the limits of the three axes identified in *Writing Degree Zero:* language or history, style or body, writing or form. These are not key terms, invariables constituting the foundation and force of a theory, but, as often happens in Barthes's conceptual groupings—connotation/denotation, pleasure/bliss, readable/writerly, *studium/punctum*—they are moments of clarification, intelligibility, they are rhetorical devices which help one think and classify on a day-to-day basis, during the transformation of a reading into writing. Barthes uses technical devices to this end; he does not pretend he is founding a sure science. It is, consequently, absurd to read the terminology of *Writing Degree Zero* with a Saussurian key, in the perspective of the *Aufhebung*, which resolves one moment with the following. It is true that after *Writing Degree Zero* Barthes was totally taken up by the structuralist wave, but even in his most obvious moments of scientific hope, his pluralism always prevented him from making any declaration of faith. Barthes's eclecticism has often attracted notice, but it is still necessary to stress it, not in order to find the volubility of theory or the fragility of a discipline, like literary criticism, linguistics, or Lacan's psychoanalytic theory, but to emphasize Barthes's loyalty to literature in its indefatigable and changing constancy. Literature always participates in various forms of knowledge and corrodes them at the same time, undermines their certainty, stages them as acts of language. In *Lecture*, his inaugural lesson for the new chair of literary semiology at the Collège de France (1978), Barthes speaks of the necessity for the writer both to shift ground and to be obstinate, basically like Michelet, who rode the waves from event to event in the vast sea of history, a voyager who made no stops, but proceeded resolutely in his work as a historian. "*To persist* means to affirm the Irreducible of literature, that which resists and survives the typified discourses, the philosophies, sciences, psychologies which surround it, to act as if literature were incomparable and immortal."[75] *To shift ground* means that the writer does not have to adhere to any standards of coherence, that he plays the games of words as far as they go, until he abjures, until he reaches the limits of histrionics. So what then could be more paradoxical than the moment in which this man, for whom the institution had created a chair of semiology, found himself speaking of the splendid mistake called literature?

A Criticism of the Imaginary

In *Michelet* Barthes's approach resembles that of the Bachelardian school of criticism: in opposition to ideological criticism, this approach which one can call criticism of the imaginary—to use a term dear to Bachelard—perceives an author—or a text—in the vortex of his own writing and seeks to retrace the birth of the very material of his creation or composition. When Barthes speaks of the organized system of Michelet's obsessions, he fulfills exactly what Jean-Pierre Richard maintained was his Bachelardian credo: "I considered the idea to be less important than the obsession, and theory secondary to the dream."[76] Barthes's reading of Michelet, a real and true critique of sensation and dream as the foundation of discourse, goes from subject to subject until it isolates the repetitive character of one of the themes—for example, the pair Guelf/Ghibelline—which organize Michelet's history into a symphony.

A thematic reading is constitutionally not ideological, and in its use of literature, stylistic thematism is similar to Foucault's idea of technology in historical analysis. It tries to find generative forces within a discourse and understand how discourses can be founded as truth; it seizes a technique at the time of its birth, rather than applying an external system, as ideological criticism does, for the very concept of ideology contains the idea of a truth that needs to be unveiled.

Someone should write a history of structuralism or of modern French criticism which would take into account its intellectual debt to Bachelard: a debt hard to recognize because Bachelard has been defined too often in terms extraneous to modernity, that is to say, of his religiosity, his complete faith in being, in human values. It is impossible for modernity and the theoretical avant-garde to recognize themselves in systems based on wholeness; it is easier to identify with any negative thinking, because it is characterized by fragmentation, bits of thought, and a crude, fundamentally discontinuous expressionism. In *Michelet*, Barthes managed to paint expressionist paintings as though the themes, or the analysis of sensations or images, could be situated either in the flow of Bachelardian imaginary or in modern fragmentation, as the detached style of Baudelaire's prose poems. In *A Lover's Discourse* he would later claim to have understood figures in their gymnastic or choreographic—and not rhetorical—sense, as though he had sought to capture the body in action, "the lover at work."[77] But in *Michelet*, he had already given the figures of history a choreographic sense, and such figures caught the historian at work, in the middle of a gesture, in the act of moving his body—one only has to read a few of the titles Barthes gave his fragments: "Michelet the Walker," "Michelet the Swimmer," "Michelet the Predator."

The link between the body and any other mental object—history, writing or style, the act of falling in love—is a theme, one of the fundamental obsessions found in Barthes's work; it is part of the organized system of obsessions he refers to in his work on Michelet. It is consequently more appropriate to examine Barthes's own obsessions, that is, to follow his style, than to follow the convolutions of his theoretical profile, linguistic or psychoanalytic, or to study the influence of Saussure or Lacan. For the obsessions lead the reader to the body as it is staged in Barthesian writing: from the mute, biological body of *Writing Degree Zero*, to the body as history in *Michelet*, to the lover's body bathed in tears in *A Lover's Discourse*, to the body of the absent mother in *Camera Lucida*. Only in this manner can we know the material that constitutes a mode of writing through time, because Roland Barthes is above all a way of writing, an author's style, and not a system, or a series of recipes. This may seem paradoxical for someone who promulgated the death of the author—a thesis which became a leitmotif of literary structuralism.[78] But beyond the provocative statements directed against any type of deterministic criticism, beyond the avant-garde tone that does away with a tradition (that of the author in literary history), if Barthes had held to Michelet he would have continued to see in death a metamorphosis; if he had held to Bachelard—whom he cites only rarely in his writings, once in his article "History or Literature?"—he would have insisted on the deforming character of images: the author and the death of the author are nothing but images, figures of the critic at work. And the figures come and go in a series of movements, of metamorphoses. And, we will see, the terrible power and at the same time impotence of images organize Barthes's note on photography, *Camera Lucida*.

Myth and History

History for Michelet is not only the body of the historian, but also the body of flesh-and-blood men who are the ultimate and essential substance of historical knowledge. From Caesar to Danton, Michelet's history is composed of a series of portraits which capture the coloring of an individual, a corporeal complexion, and not an anatomy: Louis XVI was the pallid, fat king, Robespierre was a cat, Marat a toad, and Napoleon as yellow as wax. A single stroke of the pen, and not the sum of lines or a detailed drawing, defines the historical figure as found in Michelet. Barthes affirmed in his article of 1951, "Michelet, l'Histoire et la Mort," that there is an irreducible density of the style characteristic of every writer, as of any human body in its particular traits. The bodies of the historical characters in Michelet condense the notions of style and writing in *Writing Degree Zero:* they are signs of history as well as a matter that resists history while becoming history—in short history and nonhistory at the same time, that is to say, myth. Myth, Barthes wrote in his 1951 article, is a tension "between a formal pole and a substantial pole, between categories, ends, relations, a morality, a science, a history, and bodies, real, opaque, extraordinary objects, a matter, a Poetry."[79] Before writing *Mythologies*, which concludes with a theoretical essay applying Saussurian linguistics to the Marxist dream of reading society, aiming at "a general semiology of our bourgeois world," Barthes had taken notice of Michelet's notion of the myth, of history as myth. This led him to be receptive to Lévi-Strauss's structuralism, a structuralism that should not be understood as a negation of historicism, but that cohered with the renewal of historical studies, with the new history's search for novel objects and novel methods. Michelet's own ambiguity, as well as the diffidence with which he had been perceived by positivist historians and scientists, from Taine to the Marxists, placed him in a privileged position, between history and fiction, from a structuralist viewpoint. Let us consider, for example, how audacious and equivocal *La Sorcière* (*Satanism and Witchcraft*) is: history and fiction, this book, Barthes said in his 1954 foreword, "generates a new insight into reality, initiates what we might call a historical ethnology, or a historical mythology."[80]

An ethnological or anthropological concern is constant in Barthes; it is precisely what is lacking in institutional literary history. Ethnology as a human science should account for our society which calls itself advanced, for the symbolic exchanges of our culture. As Barthes said in an interview in 1976: "There should be a kind of literary history that historians never attend to, a mythological history, covering the semicollective images of the writer within each period."[81] Then one could study Sade and Rimbaud the way Michelet kept track of the witch through the centuries: the individuality of a figure or author would be lost, but they would be seen as participants in an institutional activity which supersedes them as individuals. The function of the author, Barthes claims in "History or Literature?" would become similar to that of the sorcerer in primitive society: the sorcerer participates in the magical function, and the author in the literary one. The true object for study would be the literary function and not the individuals, even though this function is made explicit through the individuals—events and structure are not mutually exclusive. Literary history is legitimate only when it really becomes history, when it rids itself of the notion of the author, which reduces actual histories of literature to series of critical monographs and literary chronicles. One should understand that literature is an institution and study it within its institutional limits—the exercise of the literary function, the formation of the public, the mythicizing of the author.

The essay "History or Literature?" (now included in *On Racine*) was first published in 1960 in *Annales*, the journal founded by Marc Bloch and Lucien Febvre, and in that same year Barthes became a researcher in the Sixth Section (Sciences Économiques et Sociales) of the École Pratique des Hautes Études, the very institution of the historians of the *Annales*. In that article, Barthes signaled the importance for literary history of the work of Lucien Febvre, especially his *Rabelais*, precisely because it analyzes the world in which Rabelais wrote. It is not a history made of anecdotes, little facts and quarrels, but the reconstitution of an ambiance as "the locus of certain habits of thought, certain implicit taboos, certain 'natural' values, certain material interests of a group of men actually associated by identical or complementary functions—in short as a portion of a social class."[82] Rabelais is not the center of Febvre's study, but the point of departure for a discussion of the interpretations he gave rise to; he is a "crystallizer." As Lucien Febvre had said in a 1941 article, the historian must be concerned with the psychological, and must "connect, articulate the totality of conditions of existence in a given era with the meaning the men of that era gave their ideas."[83] And for the historian ideas and institutions do not come from the eternal, but from specific unrepeatable conditions. For Barthes the study of a form, or of an institution or function, includes both the generalization of the form in a model and the description of the meanings that such a form assumes, transforms, and circulates. The generalization of the form in a model corresponds to an analysis of a structuralist type, à la Lévi-Strauss, where ethnology borrows from linguistics; Barthes will use such a method later in *Mythologies* and *The Fashion System*. The description of the meanings that a form assumes, transforms, and circulates, as in analyses of a psychological kind, derived from the *Annales* school, examples of which can be found in *On Racine* and many of the *Critical Essays*.

According to Barthes, literary historians not only believe

in the eternal but unwittingly confuse two postulations which in reality belong to two different branches of study: one that is historical and institutional, and another one which resists history. The former asks questions on the meaning of ideas, while the latter escapes history because a literary work is creation, beyond any historical determinations, because it is "a hard, irreducible nut." The study of creation must necessarily be psychological. Its psychology is one of depth, one which, like the geography in which the *Annales* school was interested, reaches matter itself, arriving at the most secret layers of biology, whether it be the earth, the sea, or the body. One can now reinterpret the dual project of *Writing Degree Zero*: an attempt to indicate the institutional limits of literature and reach the material secret of creation. Then the history of writing would in reality be the sum of two different branches of study, one institutional and the other psychological: sociology and the study of the human unconscious. Such a history would answer Febvre's call for a history capable of speaking to individual sensibility and emotions, because they are social facts, existing at the base of interpersonal relationships and intellectual life. A history that would be able to record not only the nuances of sensitivity which separate generations, but also the very way in which sensitivity is created and in turn creates forms of emotions. Lucien Febvre called for a different history, which was to be written later on, at least in part: "We have no history of Love, if you think about it. We have no history of Death. We have no history of Piety or of Cruelty. We have no history of Joy."[84] This regret was probably a necessary catalyst for the decision to envisage a history of madness like Foucault's, or a history of death like the one Philippe Ariès wrote. In this same series, in spite of the Sartrean language, one must include the sketch of a history of writing that Barthes attempted in *Writing Degree Zero*.

Michelet was one of the first in the modern period to write a history that was both psychological and historical, that considered at the same time human institutions and minds, focusing on cults and obsessions, transforming itself continuously, slicing time in a way one might call vertical. *Satanism and Witchcraft* is an anthropological essay on a myth, or a theme that mutates with time; it encompasses various kinds of documents, oral as well as written, and its upsetting alchemy rises up against the immobility of a discipline, against the hierarchical separations between closed specializations: the history of witchcraft is part of the histories of France, of the church, of magic, of medicine. Lucien Febvre revaluated Michelet precisely because he was able to gather around a single problem disciplines and languages which usually ignore each other. Febvre paid little attention to the historians who have deplored Michelet's errors of documentation and his imprecision. Febvre's program for history is interdisciplinary, exactly what Barthes hoped for literary studies. Interdisciplinarity, that is, the collaboration of different disciplines, does not necessarily entail confusion, but on the contrary the capacity to make distinctions, which is exactly what literary history lacks, according to Barthes; it does not borrow from different disciplines—a discipline is not an essence, and besides, how would one draw the boundaries between various disciplines?—but brings together diverse techniques capable of interacting. This leads us back to technique. One might perhaps be able to provoke a collaboration between the most minute statistics, the most detailed type of history, and more abstract generalities, more basic structures. Only a technique of writing, a style, can merge the heterogeneous, can give a sense of transformation, metamorphosis, deformation. And what would this form be if not the form of the narrative, *mythos?*

History and the Novel

The rupture that Barthes distinguished between Balzac and Flaubert is the beginning of modernity, and the nineteenth century is the one that invented history and the novel. This is to say that it gave them a new meaning and an institutional force: I am using "invent" in Foucault's sense, and referring to the discovery of a technique, not of a substance. Iron, for example, had always existed, but the new technology of iron permitted the construction of the railways in the nineteenth century. The writing of the novel, in the nineteenth century, was founded on the narrative, exactly the way history was: other epochs conceived the novel in the form of letters, for instance. History can be therefore conceived as something different from the narration of facts, and one can envisage history as analysis.

The narrative is the form that validated history and literature in a particular period, and this brings us back to Michelet, the historian whose tale telling follows a dual movement. The first sees history as a current the historian closely follows, going from event to event in a quick run or in a slow, majestic stride; the second focuses on the picture, the glance that takes in the entire scene. In other words, event and structure: before the rise of structuralist language the two instances coexisted without excluding each other. Time is sliced in two directions. One is flowing, diachronic, the other is structural, synchronic. In *Michelet*, Barthes understands narrativity as having a double constitution. This would be denied later by the structuralist credo Barthes adopted, in 1966, in his famous article in *Communications*, "Structural Analysis of Narratives," where narrativity is studied only as a series of synchronic sequences.[85]

Above all it is interesting to note that, by means of narration, the use of the past tense and the first person, the novel and history share the same rhetoric: facts—what really happened, what can be documented—and fiction—the aura of verisimilitude that supports the novel—are two sides of the same coin. Michelet is to be found exactly at the crossroads between truth and verisimilitude, and this fusion is brought about by his obsessive insistence on morality, the truth-value which precedes the fact. The separation of these two aspects of the narrative—truth versus fiction, or reality versus verisimilitude—is the exigency of another, nonexplicit rhetoric, of an undeclared morality which precedes the facts: that of objectivity, of the scientific approach, of documentation, where the written document is preferred to the oral one. But Michelet preferred the oral one because it is voice, and voice belongs to the human body, to the bodies of the people he wished to resuscitate.

History, before it became an autonomous science, was part of eloquence, of the art of persuasion, and today, even when, as in numerous cases with new history, it renews narrative form, it seems to want to conceal its own rhetoric, its wish to be, in every case, the writing of the *real*, the document of the event that has actually taken place. But one must ask whether it is legitimate to draw a distinction between fictional and historical narratives. Is discourse that claims to be founded on reality *truly* different from imaginary discourse? As Barthes pointed out in "The Discourse of History,"[86] Nietzsche was suspicious of the notion of historical fact, because it does not exist in itself: one needs to create meaning in order to give existence to the fact. The fact is therefore first endowed with a linguistic existence, like personal pronouns, which, as Émile Benveniste said, are first of all terms of discourse, linguistic instances, and not essences.

The actual state of history is not so much one of being conceived as finalized history, or of finding itself in a new scientific era, as one of continuing to legitimize itself as the study of the real. And this requires a certain blindness regarding the foundations of historical discourse, the fact that history, before being history, is language. For example, Paul Veyne, one of the spokesmen for the new history in France, criticizes both the "ingenuity and rigidity of Marxist concepts" in the study of history and the "chatter" of purely narrative history. While justly upholding the necessity for concepts and suggesting "an ideal history of humanity, in which the chapters would not have as title 'The Orient, Greece, The Middle Ages,' but 'From Power by Subjective Right to Power by Delegation.'"[87] Veyne does not dwell on the fact that even these terms are part of a rhetoric. But perhaps this is a literary problem. If so, one probably should not study the relationships between history and the other human sciences—sociology, economics, etc.—but one should investigate instead the relationship between history and literature, and restudy the nineteenth century in this perspective. Thus, just as rewriting the history of literature requires one to account for the historicity of literature, of its being an object, so, in order to write history, one must not forget its literarity, its rhetorical side (a telling fact: in France, Lanson, the founder of literary history, held the chair of French eloquence at the Sorbonne).

The substance of history, like that of literature, is certainly language. And language is a structure, a structure made not only of linguistic events, but also of those real events that language wishes to represent, to organize, or to exclude. Language and reality face each other. One can believe that language represents reality—that is, the discourse of realism, of history, of ideology, and of the critique of ideology—or, on the other hand, one can believe that the only true reality is language, an omnistructuring structure, an absolute form which engulfs subjects, the world, and society—this is the structuralist assumption. Structuralism, the new science of language, triumphant in France after the war in Algeria, seems to respond to an old hope, that of universalizing language, of finding general and secure models. It was born of a very modern feeling, that it is impossible to dominate all of reality, to know or control it in its increasingly overwhelming plurality. Therefore, Barthes's first paradox regards history, because history emerges as the deep obsession of one of the founders of French structuralism, which has been perceived as nonhistorical or antihistorical. This paradox leads undoubtedly to a second one, one that deals with language, and I shall argue that Barthes does not simply worship language, but also hates it. *Odi et amo*, such is the paradox of the true lover.

Je suis obligé de parler. Je ne me tairai jamais. Jamais?—Samuel
Beckett, *L'Innommable*

A Passion for Signs

Structuralism is nothing but a historical phenomenon.
Barthes had been aware of this since 1963:

> Structuralism does not withdraw history from the
> world: it seeks to link to history not only certain con-
> tents (this has been done a thousand times) but also
> certain forms, not only the material but also the intel-
> ligible, not only the ideological, but also the aesthetic.
> And precisely because all thought about the histor-
> ically intelligible is also a participation in that intel-
> ligibility, structural man is scarcely concerned to last;
> he knows that structuralism, too, is a certain form of
> the world, which will change with the world; and just
> as he experiences his validity (but not his truth) in his
> power to speak the old languages of the world in a new

way, so he knows that he will suffice that a new language rise out of history, a new language which speaks *him* in his turn, for his task to be done.[1]

If one were to try to determine which terms recur most frequently in Barthes's work, one would certainly find that the word "language" is one of the most often used. It is, in fact, a word that characterizes the entire *episteme* of the twentieth century. One day, perhaps (and that day may have already arrived), the phrases which have made history will appear in their full rhetorical density. Then we will cease looking for true ideas; we will stop exploring all the philosophical ramifications of every word. We will instead look at these terms understanding that they bear witness to the obsessions of certain specific periods and intellectual groups.

They will not lend themselves to explanations or to further development, but will simply resonate like Michelet's themes. They will be tonal rather than conceptual words, insistent images in the gnoseological portrait of a given period. Let us think, for example, of what the term "science" meant for the positivist era. Then Lacan's famous words, "The unconscious is structured like a language," will not seem that different from Renan's "The future is science."

And yet, our age, which has praised language, is profoundly antirhetorical. The age of the city is over but the metropolis is booming. Eloquence—the living word capable of persuasion, the dialogical and political word—has been devalued.[2] The century of linguistics and psychoanalysis—the most advanced segments of which have, as Lacanian analysis has, reread Freud from a linguistic perspective—has rejected rhetoric. Our century, which has seen the development of communications systems, began by demonstrating its distrust of language—Lord Chandos's silence is one example. Barthes expressed disgust for the rhetorical fabric of language, its arena, "constructed like a football field": "Language is the field of *Mache: pugna ver-*

borum. There is a whole dossier to be collected—a book to be written: that of the governed contestations of language; they are always regulated: in language, nothing is ever wild, primitive, everything is coded, even and especially trial of strength: Sophistics, *Disputatio*, *Hain-Tenys*, political confrontations, today's intellectual debates."[3]

Even the structuralist emphasis on the *signifiant* (signifier) is a symptom of a distrust in language as it is understood by rhetoric, i.e., as communication among people and persuasion. *Signifiant:* the word is so sonorous in its use of the present participle, but remains indeterminate because it is both empty of specific meaning and capable of carrying several meanings. The present participle suggests, but it does not persuade. Ancient rhetoric believes that language and reality are in a harmonious relationship, while modern theories believe that language and reality cannot adjust to each other. For example, Lacan's conception of the primacy of the letter,[4] or Derrida's insistence on the notion of writing, is not simply an attempt to liberate that which, since Plato, has been repressed for numerous centuries in western culture: the signifier, writing, because "the history of truth, of the truth of truth, has always been . . . the debasement of writing and its repression outside 'full' speech."[5] The age of computers marks a deep turmoil in what Derrida calls the great metaphysical adventure of western thought. The time has come to see that the signifier and writing are not devoid of meaning, but can produce a multiplicity of meanings. The time has come to break with the implications of our logocentric culture. Derrida writes:

> All signifiers, and first and foremost the written signifier, are derivative with regard to what would wed the voice indissolubly to the mind or to the thought of the signified sense, indeed to the thing itself (whether it is done in the Aristotelian manner that we have just indicated or in the manner of medieval theology, deter-

mining the *res* as a thing created from its *eidos*, from its sense thought in the logos or in the infinite understanding of God). The written signifier is always technical and representative. It has no constitutive meaning. This derivation is the very origin of the notion of the "signifier." The notion of sign always implies within itself the distinction between signifier and signified, even if, as Saussure argues, they are distinguished simply as the two faces of one and the same leaf. This notion remains therefore within the heritage of that logocentrism which is also a phonocentrism: absolute proximity of voice and being, of voice and the meaning of being, of voice and the ideality of being.[6]

The contemporary emphasis on the signifier as the producer of meanings appears as the historical symptom of a troubled relationship between reality and language, presupposing the single historical split of modernity which began in the middle of the nineteenth century, as though modern thinkers had seen the birth of new problems whereas all other eras had done nothing but repeat the same formulas. This is the trap that the avant-garde since the romantics have fallen into, believing in the absolute newness of an experience. Michel Foucault's contribution has been essential here, for he managed not to privilege modernity by determining other historical breaks and exploring the productive as well as repressive value of the interplay between power and knowledge.[7]

Where exactly can we situate Barthes in the continuum which runs from praise to distrust of language? We find him at that extreme point where subjectivity does not communicate with society, with any social language, a point which indicates the fundamental disharmony between language and reality, the former being unidimensional, the latter being multidimensional. From Baudelaire and Flaubert to Barthes, such is the historical genealogy. At that point the ultimate refuge is to be found in literature, almost in art for art's sake—minus the programmatic belief in such a formula.[8] Literature stays then at the farthest away from rhetoric: cut away from society, from the *polis*, from the *pugna verborum*. Rhetoric is language offered to the world, literature is language subtracted from the world.

The terms "writing," "*langue*," "language," "style" are therefore frequent in Barthes's texts: they come and they go, bearing variable and ambiguous meanings which follow the very particular course of Barthesian semiology. The semiological *doxa* must certainly honor Barthes for having introduced into literary criticism themes and problems which originated in Saussure's linguistics and in Lacan's psychoanalysis with its structuralist orientation. On the other hand, a paradoxical reading of his works inevitably highlights the way his writing was firmly rooted in a rebellion against language—and "against" is used here in its double sense of antagonism as well as proximity and physical closeness. *Contra* is the preposition of both hatred and love. In that case all of Barthes's work will appear to be a hand-to-hand combat with language—the same battle that forms the basis of *Writing Degree Zero*, where we saw the writer struggling to extricate his writing from the physicality of language, from the rigidity of linguistic codes. Writing goes against natural language, against the language spoken by one's contemporaries. Thus, in *Roland Barthes*, that critical autobiography made of textual fragments which challenges both autobiography and criticism as genres, Barthes asks himself, "and what if all his life *he had chosen the wrong language?* He is all the more readily overcome by this panic here (in U.) where, staying home at night, he watches television a good deal: here is continually represented (remonstrated) a public language from which he is separated; this language interests him, but this interest is not reciprocal: to the television public, his own language would seem entirely unreal (and outside aesthetic delight, any unreal language is likely to be ridiculous)."[9]

Here we come up against one of the most complex problems of literary semiology, and of all structuralism: the
split between written and oral language. How can linguistics and literature be compared when the first has oral
language as its point of reference and the second written
language? In *Writing Degree Zero* Barthes maintained that
"all modes of writing have in common the fact of being
'closed' and thus different from spoken language,"[10] and he
maintained later on, in 1971, that "Jakobson made literature a magnificent gift: he gave it linguistics. Of course,
literature did not wait to know it was Language: all of classical Rhetoric, until Valéry, attests to the fact."[11] Saussure
had, of course, already come across the stumbling block of
written and oral language, and, as Derrida pointed out, he
spoke in chapter 6 of his *Cours* of "the tyranny of the letter."[12] Out of that difficulty there emerged two Saussures:
the author of the notes later collected in the *Cours de linguistique générale* and the author of the *Anagrammes*.[13]
One determined the fundamental law of the linearity of
oral language, which travels from the mouth of the speaker
to the ear of the listener. The other, while studying ancient
Latin poetry in which the verses both ran forward in a linear fashion and turned back on themselves, discovered a
law opposite to the law of linguistics. Under the words
there were other words. The repetition of initials reproduced the names of the heroes or gods to whom the
poems were secretly dedicated. There is an abyss between
written and oral language because both oral and written—
literary or poetic—languages create meaning in totally different ways. This abyss can be bridged, however, because
the generalized science of signs, semiology as it is defined
by both Saussure and Jakobson, is not so much a science of
communication as it is one of signification, and, as Jakobson said, the poetic function is inherent in the use of spoken language. Barthes echoes Jakobson's thinking when he
maintains that "every speech-act which accentuates the
form of the message is poetic."[14] But ambiguity remains, as

does the paradox that linguistics, which concerns itself with oral language, is a written science. Derrida's attempts, in the 1960s and 1970s, to constitute a grammatology and establish the primacy of writing can be interpreted as part of a general effort to resolve this ambiguity. He suggested that oral language not only appears to be written, but that it has perhaps always been so, and that the entire emphasis our culture places on voice, the *logos*, the presence of the word, stems from a great repression of writing begun by Plato when he relegated it to being a copy of a copy. The passage from the primacy of the voice to that of writing is symptomatic of malaise; the belief that one has found a solution, though it may be negative, and that one can sweep away the errors of the past is typical of the avant-garde. But what if the two possibilities existed without there being a primacy of one or the other? What if there were a continual coming and going, an eternal return but never a winner? or irregular cycles, passages, emanations, images, figures in the state of becoming?

Barthesian semiology organized and disorganized itself in a movement analogous to that of figures found in the lover's discourse which passes from resistance to exaltation and to weariness. But the three stages become one, because they do not lead one into another in a logical or chronological manner, but move together in a kind of dance. In short, Barthesian semiology is a passion. Gérard Genette had understood this when, in the early 1960s, he remarked on Barthes's diversified imagery, which borrows from Marxism, Bachelard, and the *Nouveau Roman*, and on his "conversion" to structuralism as being of superficial importance: "Barthesian semiology, in its origin and in its active principle, is characterized by a man fascinated by signs: this fascination has without a doubt a good portion of repulsion mixed into it, as was the case with Flaubert and Baudelaire, and has the essentially ambiguous character of a passion."[15]

It is a passion which distinguishes between "good" signs

and "bad" ones. A good sign reveals its arbitrary character immediately, whereas a bad one tries to pass for natural. The well-known example given by Barthes in *Mythologies* is that of the black soldier on the cover of *Paris-Match:* his saluting the French flag is made to seem sincere. How can we doubt the goodness of the French empire when this Algerian appears to be, like any other Frenchman, proud to be part of it?[16] Barthes's structuralism is, as Genette explains, quite far from being an abandonment of responsibility vis-à-vis meaning. It is far from being pure formalism. On the contrary—Genette argues—it is extremely moral, a kind of catharsis, which uncovers the true meaning of things on the other side of myth and unmasks the ways in which history distorts meanings. For Barthes, myth has a double meaning. On the one hand—and this is its positive side—it is the constant formation of images out of matter, as in Michelet; rich and poetic, it recalls Vico's vision of the creative activity of humankind at the early stages of civilization. On the other hand—and this is its negative value—it is both an ideological incrustation and evidence of an imposture. Barthes's semiology intends to break the ideological incrustation of myths. Semiological analysis collides with the world of communication—the press, the cinema, fashion, advertising—which can be defined as the world of oral language, as well as with the world of literature, which is the world of written language: in *Mythologies* Barthes maintained that *Writing Degree Zero* "was nothing but a mythology of literary language,"[17] that is to say, an analysis of the signs literature uses to define itself as such. But behind the institution of literature, which necessarily implies ideology, negative myths, glimmers literature itself, the real thing. Genette points out what can be called Barthes's nostalgia for literature. The movement from the signified to the signifier is only superficially a dismissal of meaning: "We should rather say that it goes from the ideological sense, which is an abusive word to the poetic sense, which is a silent presence."[18] Genette almost anticipates the last phase of Barthes's development when, in his inaugural lecture at the Collège de France, Barthes stated: "Literary semiology is, as it were, that journey which lands us in a country free by default; angels and dragons are no longer there to defend it."[19] The semiologist hides the poet of Hofmannsthal, his eyes without eyelids, constantly open upon any aspect of the world.

Style and Writing

The three stages of passion—resistance, exaltation, and weariness—can be used to describe the path followed by the relationship between writing and language as it was developed from *Writing Degree Zero* to "Inaugural Lecture."

Barthes says in *Roland Barthes* that he has an illness: "I *see* language."[20] He sees it in the way Werther saw Charlotte with Albert and was wounded. Language is owned by others. It is assailed and undermined by stereotypes. Barthes, like Flaubert, is obsessed by the idea that language can be worn out. This takes us back to the fundamental discourse of *Writing Degree Zero*, besides its being a mythology of literary language: only the invention of a writing, of a language, can free one from linguistic wearing out, can enable one to escape from that which language, as the circulation of signs, the law of power, forces one to say, because language, like money, is a symbolic structure which regulates the relationships among men, taking the form of particular languages or linguistic systems. In order to free oneself from the erosion of language one must invent a fresh new language, one must disregard cultural souvenirs, the weight of tradition, and the tics of the avantgarde. Because of its using up, language resists the writer: the cost of form is high and those who write must struggle with that deaf and abused matter that is language. It is also the using up of language which sets the scene for the weariness of stereotypes, the horror of repetition, and the rejection of congealed forms and ideas.

In order to prevent language from wearing out, writers would have to be—always and tirelessly—*logothetes*. Barthes uses this term to name the founders of artificial languages which explode natural language. Sade, Fourier, and Loyola founded such languages when they produced, on the other side of sadism, revolution, and mysticism, texts that were similar in their linguistic freshness, characterized by similar combinations, and animated by a similar desire to classify and eagerness to enumerate. *Sade, Fourier, Loyola* is a happy book, borne of the pleasure of reading, the pleasure of the text, of the very notion of a text, the text being a new object, which takes the place of the traditional notion of a work. In a 1971 article, "From Work to Text," Barthes said: "The work is a fragment of substance, it occupies a portion of the spaces of books (for example, in a library). The Text is a methodological field . . . the work is held in the hand, the text is held in language: it exists only when caught up in a discourse."[21] Not only did the text signal the possibility of overcoming the dichotomy between written language and oral language (or, at least, the dichotomy between good and bad literature): one can find a little bit of text everywhere. The text is plural and attains "if not the transparency of social relations, at least the transparency of language relations: it is the space in which no language prevails over any other, where the languages circulate (retaining the *circular* meaning of the word)."[22]

Thanks to those who have been able to found new languages, thanks to the force of the text, the semiological dream seems to have come true: though we may not be able to overcome class structure in the social world, we are, however, able to do so in the pleasure of reading, in the agreement of those familiar with the pleasure obtained from a light, happy writing. The same exaltation results from a taste for new languages and from the evidence that the languages of the *logothetes*—Sade, Fourier, Loyola, and anyone else who invents a language—cannot but be open "to the semiological definition of the Text."[23] It is a real and true festival, like the joy of the subject in love who experiences every encounter with the beloved as ecstatic, as Barthes writes in *A Lover's Discourse*.[24] It is the perfect meeting of a theory of the text, which provoked numerous debates in France in the 1960s and 1970s, and a practice of the text, the writing of Sade, Fourier, and Loyola. The critic, like the lover, experiences the exaltation of the harmony between intellectual research and the passion for reading. Everything coincides, and fusion takes place: a fusion between reading and writing, between theory and practice, between the written and spoken word, between critical and poetic writing. Fusion is a festival, the very principle of bliss.

The struggle of writing against the resistance of language becomes a festival only when the product of such a struggle can be found in reading, that is to say, in the contact with a new, young writing that has broken with tradition, with imposed stereotypes and codes.

Speaking of writing, language, and style in *Sade, Fourier, Loyola*, Barthes uses Lacan's terminology ("consistency," "insistency"):

> Although all three are committed, through historical position, to an ideology of representation and sign, what our logothetes produce is nonetheless already text; that is to say, that for platitude of style (as found in "great" writers), they have found a way to substitute volume of writing. The style supposes and practices the opposition of matter and form; it is the lamination of a substructure; the writing reaches a point at which it produces a row of signifiers, such that no language matter can still be recovered; because it is conceived as a "form," style implies a "consistency"; the writing, to use Lacan's term, only recognizes "instances."[25]

One thing seems made for the other: the *logothete* for a semiology of the text and vice versa, and literature for psychoanalysis and vice versa. Here style appears to be that which has a consistency; it has the properties of language and of weight. It recalls that which has been fixed by tradition: the system, the novel, and the oration—such are the genres in which the three *logothetes* have been frozen by the history of literature. But a festival implies fusion, and then, little by little, "as the style is absorbed into the writing," the system, the novel, and oration become dissolved in something that is systematic, novelistic, fantastic, and ends up being very different from the system, the novel, and oration. This something is a flavor and not any longer a category: "Sade is no longer an erotic, Fourier no longer a utopian, Loyola no longer a saint."[26]

Absorption and dissolution are the very opposites of consistency and weight. They oppose resistance, or rather, they result from a victory over the resistance of natural language and stereotypes (*stereos* means solid)—dense, hard matter: one has to insist in order to break resistance, one has to persist in writing in order to find new writing.[27]

We know that the terms "style" and "writing," together with those of "*langage*" and "*langue*," had been used in *Writing Degree Zero* in a different way and without reference to the ideas of Lacan and Saussure, with which Barthes was not yet familiar. Style, conceived as the very body of the writer, certainly had weight, but did not appear negative. It was almost a mute value, but pliable, like formless matter, to the requirements of what had been defined as a formal value—writing. But in *Sade, Fourier, Loyola*, it is the style of the great writers recognized by literary history that is consistent, like a negative value: it has all the weight of language, of a *langue* that is codified and transmitted, and it must evaporate, be absorbed into writing. In an article that appeared almost simultaneously with *Sade, Fourier, Loyola*, Barthes pointed out that style "has always been part of a binary system, or, if you prefer, in a mythological paradigm of two terms" which "naturally have changed names and even content, according to periods and schools."[28] As Barthes maintains in "Style and Its Image," the older opposition is that of *Content* and *Form*, founded on the rhetorical opposition between *res* and *verba*. The more recent opposition, which comes from Saussurian linguistics, is between norm (*la norme*) and deviance (*l'écart*): "Style is then seen as the exception (though coded) to a rule; it is the (individual, yet institutional) aberration of a current usage, sometimes perceived as verbal (if we define the norm by the spoken language), sometimes as prosaic (if we set Poetry in opposition to 'something else')."[29] In the article "Style and Its Image," Barthes's position remains ambiguous, in the sense that he defines style in the terms of linguistics, as adopted by the mythologist: "The stylistic system, which is one system among others, has a function of naturalization, or of familiarization, or of domestication . . . What is more familiar, more obvious, more natural, than a sentence read? Style 'overspreads' the semantic articulations of content; by metonymic means, it naturalizes the story told, declares it innocent."[30]

In the end this negativity of style is not very important. Barthes is actually arguing against the image of style using Jakobson's techniques and terminologies. What matters is that here Barthes addresses the main issue of the difference between written and spoken language. He believes that if, in modern terms, style rests on the opposition between norm and deviance, then style as literary effect is perceived as an aberrant message which violates, or takes by surprise, the current code of spoken language. Style ends up being distant, different from the type of language considered normal. This is an unfortunate difference founded on something very evident: spoken language, on the one hand, develops in a linear movement of sentences, which are very often unfinished, and which, therefore, are not sentences. Written language, on the other hand, is characterized by closed, concluded sentences (Barthes used to say that a professor is someone who, when speaking, finishes his sentences).[31] However, the object of linguistics is the sentence: one almost needs to have two autonomous linguistics, one of oral, the other of written, sentences. But if one were to institute these two sciences, one would be adhering to the philosophy that separates speech and writing and denounces the paradoxical position that linguistics assumes when it concerns itself with written language, while simultaneously pretending that the canonical form of language is the live word and writing is nothing but the transcription of it.

Barthes could not resolve the problem, he could only indicate how complicated it is. He could not surmount the opposition between norm and deviance, between written and oral language. Not unlike Raymond Queneau, Barthes was puzzled by this opposition, but he did not try to destroy it, as Queneau tried to do with his works written according to the pronunciation, grammar, and syntax of spoken French. But Barthes read into the problem of written and oral language all possible implications and came to postulate the abstractness of literary language—the very institution of style—which precedes any choice of individual style. In short, he is concerned with the way in which the myth of style became a myth. The idea itself of style is an image, a stereotype.

This brings us back to the analysis of mythologies. The fact is that when Barthes immersed himself completely in linguistics, when he looked at literature from a linguistic point of view, he behaved as a sociologist, as a mythologist, or simply as a critic of ideology. He became caught in the duplicity of the critic of ideology who seeks to tear through the veil of illusions which we all create with the very language of these illusions; he was forced to hope for a science to come which would be able to speak the whole truth and liberate the sign from its fundamental alienation, which lies in the division between the signifier and the signified, and in the idea that there are "natural" meanings.

But the festival does not reside in any future science, it exists in a completely private and personal moment: the bliss or pleasure of the text. The festival implies the liberty of an individual who does not let himself be frightened by the bugbear of logical contradiction: "Such a man would be the mockery of our society: court, school, asylum, polite conversation would cast him out: who endures contradiction without shame? Now this anti-hero exists: he is the reader of the text at the moment he takes pleasure. Thus the Biblical myth is reversed, the confusion of tongues is no longer a punishment, the subject gains access to bliss by the cohabitation of languages *working side by side:* the text of pleasure is a sanctioned Babel."[32]

It is a truly erotic, Dionysian moment, which recalls Nietzsche and Bataille, rather than Lacan, though *The Pleasure of the Text* does situate itself in a Lacanian context through its use of terminology and the coupling of *jouissance* (bliss) and *plaisir* (pleasure). Barthes posits a fundamental opposition between desire and the law, pleasure and the institution, while Lacan cannot conceive of one without the other. In this regard Barthes differs also from Blanchot, though he resembles him in many other ways. For Blanchot, the law will never be reducible to the institution. Consider, for example, *La Folie du jour*, a story which distinguishes the law from the institution, showing the oppressive character of the latter, whereas the law appears as nonoppressive. The institution is, in fact, represented by the doctors who, like policemen, try to force the narrator, who has been mysteriously blinded, to explain how the accident occurred. The law, on the other hand, appears in the guise of a woman: "Behind their backs [the doctors'], I caught the silhouette of the law. Not the law commonly known, that is, rigorous and disagreeable: this one was quite different. I was far from being felled by its threat; instead it was I who terrified it. I would have thought my glance was fulminating and my hands were occasions of death."[33] The allegorical figure of the law acts as the double of the narrator, as his deepest being, his ego: "The truth is that we can no longer be separated. I will follow you everywhere, I will live under your roof, we will share the same sleep."[34]

In order for there to be a festival, one must turn one's

back on all social constraints. The festival implies reading, or writing, in which one discovers the pleasure of writing experienced by the *logothetes*, by those who exploded the opposition between norm and deviance. While the new science was failing to give rules for a perfect society, Barthes was developing the classical, ancient taste for hedonism. In a 1977 interview he lamented that hedonism had been excluded from our society: "Hedonism is considered 'bad.' Not nice. Poorly understood. It's unbelievable how pejorative this word can get. No one, no one at all, no philosophy, no doctrine, dares to take up hedonism. It's an 'obscene' word."[35]

The privileged object of hedonism is for Barthes without a doubt the text: a site that admits plurality, coexistence, fascination, and the happy coincidence of the book and life: "The index of the pleasure of the Text, then, is when we are able to live with Fourier, with Sade."[36] The text is a space freed from ideology, even from any avant-garde ideology, like that of the death of the author. The author and his works are the touchstones of traditional literary history and criticism, and the text in avant-garde theory represents the end of the traditional biographical constraint of the author and his works. But the pleasure of the text rejects both traditional and avant-garde rules: "The pleasure of the text also includes the amicable return of the author";[37] the text constitutes a place outside of the institution, outside of knowledge established as discipline and dogma: "Nothing is more depressing than to imagine the Text as an intellectual object."[38]

But the text and style are not always different for Barthes. It is not always the case that one resides in plurality and the other in the binary opposition between norm and deviation. In fact, in *Roland Barthes*, style becomes a positive value, a value which leads to the ideal of the fragment and lets the writer unburden himself of his "reactive" tendencies: "In what he writes, there are two texts. Text I is reactive, moved by indignations, fears, unspoken rejoinders, minor paranoias, defenses, scenes. Text II is active, moved by pleasure. But as it is written, corrected, accommodated to the fiction of Style, Text I becomes active too, whereupon it looses its reactive skin, which subsists only in patches (mere parentheses)."[39] Here "text" is not capitalized, but "Style" is. As for the indignation, the fears, defenses, and scenes, all these inner reactions are nothing but the secret biology of the body, and, therefore, in the language of *Writing Degree Zero*, the style of a writer.

Voice

Why does Barthes oscillate between a negative and a positive evaluation of style? What advantage could this inconstancy have, Barthes's own intentions aside? The ambiguity between writing and style is valuable in that it displaces the classical distinction between *langue* and *parole* which allowed Saussure to give a noteworthy freedom to the speaker, who is free to borrow words from an already existing linguistic system. His choice is determined only by his own desires and the concrete situation in which he is expressing himself. Barthes places the problem of liberty and constraint in the context of the tearing condition of the writer, in written and not in oral language. Faced with the blank page, the writer can no longer play the game a speaker plays when he chooses his words almost spontaneously, fancifully, with a kind of physical immediacy, without worrying about finishing his sentences. The written word creates a system that is heavier than spoken language. It must always come to terms with history and tradition. I have already said that, in the end, white writing or the utopia of language is not possible because history always wins out: it engulfs, swallows all forms by institutionalizing them, or forgetting them completely.

Furthermore, the Barthesian indecision between writing and style justifies the presence of the voice in writing. In *The Pleasure of the Text*, Barthes says that the moment of perfect pleasure lies in writing out loud, in vocal writing and not in oral or rhetorical language, language in the very *actio* of discourse. On the contrary, writing out loud is carried by the word without discourse, by pure voice, "the grain of the voice, which is an erotic mixture of timbre and language."[40] In short, it marks the beginning of the body. But the body of the text, of the author who, in the pleasure of the text, reappears in an intimate way, that body can only be style, as in *Writing Degree Zero*, a particular, individual style, a style that is anonymous because immersed in biology. Solitude, which in *Writing Degree Zero*, as I have argued in the first chapter, forms the basis of a writer's style, transforms its tragic overtones and returns in the explosion of pleasure. It returns in the text's tissue of multiplicity, in the flickering created by variation—*moire*, a tissue that changes color, serves as an image which Barthes uses frequently to signify the text. Though it may be a solitude of responsibility and fear, of incommunicability as an existential condition, it is also euphoric like the solitude of incommunicable pleasure, of bliss. One should not put too much stress on the difference between bliss (*jouissance*) and pleasure (*plaisir*), though Lacanian orthodoxy imposes it, because both are emotions: "Emotion: why should it be antipathetic to bliss (I was wrong when I used to see it wholly on the side of sentimentality, of moral illusion)? . . . Against the general rule: *never allow oneself to be deluded by the image of bliss*."[41] Of the many statements on the asocial character of pleasure in *The Pleasure of the Text*, the following will suffice as example:

> I love the text because for me it is that rare locus of language from which any "scene" (in the household, conjugal sense of the term), any logomachy is absent. The text is never a "dialogue": no risk of feint, of aggression, of blackmail, no rivalry of idiolects; the text establishes a sort of islet within the human—the common—relation, manifests the asocial nature of plea-

sure (only leisure is social), grants a glimpse of the scandalous truth about bliss: that it may well be, once the image-reservoir of speech is abolished, *neuter.*[42]

Anguish and bliss, in Freud as in Lacan, go together, pursue each other in a continuous *fort-da*, in an avoidable and rhythmic alternation.

In the voice in writing, the sound-voice of Joyce, lies the rediscovery of the body in its most mysterious, least rationalizable dimension. Language is rediscovered as body. The voice in writing, or writing aloud, searches for "the language lined with flesh, a text where we can hear the grain of the throat, the patina of consonants, the voluptuousness of vowels, a whole carnal stereophony."[43] Here lies the perfection of literature, that which makes it a song, music: the voice, mysteriously taken from a person, both particular to a body and anonymous like matter in its primordial state, this voice is integrated into what is by nature mute, the written page. In this way literature can give us pleasure in something which is absent but present in its absence, because this writing out loud is not read with the sound of a voice, but is imagined as vocal, perceived as a voice that is all the more beautiful for not being real, for being the memory of a voice, the physical perception of the vocal possibility of written language.

The Platonic background is undeniable. For, at the moment of pleasure, we see a return of the modern distrust of language as meaning, as communication. Barthes says that he hears in this writing out loud "the articulation of the body, of the tongue, not that of meaning, of language."[44] In short, the articulation of something more real, more intense than language. But *articulation* is a property of language, of speech itself. How can one believe in a domain beyond language if all the pleasure of the text is said to come out of the word, in written language, in complete sentences, or in some subversive sentence that has been left in suspense, continued in a question that is already an answer, or restrained in parentheses, or in a series of colons or dots? What else is this if not the literary style authorized by modernity, by Mallarmé's *Coup de dés?* Once again Barthes finds himself in the position of Hofmannsthal. Like Lord Chandos he can only write the impossibility of language, and like the traveler on his return he must express *in words* the intensity of an experience, whether it be the truth of Van Gogh's painting, the intensity of color, or the charm of a voice or melody. But Barthes can only express euphoria relative to language, in a search for the silent voice, because writing aloud is not a practice, a technique like the *actio* in ancient rhetoric. Its aim is not the expressivity of discourse, the clarity of the linguistic message, the theatrical aspect of communication which allows a more direct contact between one individual and another. Writing aloud is connected with the ungraspable reality of the body, of matter, of desires. It is language caught in its primordial physical aspect—throat, voice, mouth, "a whole carnal stereophony"—without all the rules of syntax, of grammar upon which human exchanges rely. It is a writing that one can talk about "as though it existed."[45] *As though it existed:* it is, therefore, presence and absence, voice and writing, imagined and real. It is, in short, something that does not admit oppositions as exclusions, but integrates them all.

But above all, the voice that one can speak of as though it existed takes us back to Michelet, to his formidable work as a historian who tried to give history a voice or many voices, the voices of the dead who have made history. Barthes wrote in *Michelet:*

> For Michelet the historical mass is not a puzzle to reconstitute, it is a body to embrace. The historian exists only to recognize a warmth . . . The roots of historical truth are therefore the documents as voices, not as witnesses. Michelet considers in them, exclusively, that quality of having been an attribute of life, the privi-

leged object to which clings a kind of residual memory of past bodies. Thus, the closer a document comes to a voice, the less it departs from the warmth which has produced it, and the more it is the true foundation of historical credibility.[46]

This is exactly the sensuality of *The Pleasure of the Text*, the materiality of the voice *in absentia*, and in spite of absence. It corresponds to the ideal of beautiful writing, that is, of writing that gives pleasure: voice and writing should "be as fresh, supple, lubricated, delicately granular and vibrant as an animal's muzzle."[47] Finally, writing should have the heat of the body, of breath. Barthes suggests that pleasure, or bliss, is far from what he condemned in his article "Style and Its Image," from "the humanist myth of living sentences, effluvium of an organic model."[48] *Organicity* is absolutely opposed to modernist taste and experience. Not organicity, but the *organ* is valorized by Barthes: the lips, the mouth, the ears. For we are dealing here with a fragmentary organicity, with the pleasure of fetishism. A baby's first experience of his body is fragmentary; therefore, when one seeks pleasure one is trying to find an infancy that is either forgotten or incompatible with the pact of meaning and reason that is desired by our society and culture.

The theme of the written voice (or of vocal writing) produces another important shift in Saussurian linguistics. The linguist conceives of a simple separation between the active subject who speaks and the passive subject who listens. We ought, instead, to consider that when we listen, we not only receive the voice of the other, but we also wander mentally, thanks to our own silent voice enclosed within the body, thanks to interior language, a language that is not composed by full sentences, but is fragmentary, like oral language. When we wander, we follow individual associations, which do not differ much from those that a text of pleasure provokes when it makes us lift our eyes from the page and think of something else. One can also engage in a dialogue with the one who is speaking while he is speaking, and thus create the condition by which interlocution will become allocution, the sonorous voice at the moment in which one is about to speak. Such is the game of the *I* and *you* of which Émile Benveniste speaks[49]: these pronouns are instances of discourse, and not definite essences, full subjects. We know how much Benveniste fascinated Barthes, for the precise reason that he succeeded in placing "the subject (in the philosophic sense of the word) in the center of the great categories of language, showing, in the case of extremely diverse phenomena [the middle sounds of Indo-European verbs, the structure of personal pronouns, the system of verbal tenses in French] that this subject can never be distinguished from an 'instance of discourse,' unlike the instance of reality."[50] This is to say that Benveniste founded the identity between subject and language.

To be against language means to explore all possibilities and use writing to reject the very foundations of Saussurian linguistics. Then there would no longer be an active subject and a passive subject, one who speaks and one who listens, there would no longer be a codified dialogue, but a vocal drama, as in the fragments of a lover's discourse. There would no longer be a precise separation between the person who says *I* and the person who says *you*, since *I* and *you* can be turned inside out, like a glove, as they pass from one mouth to another. Instead, there would be the dramatic simultaneity of personal pronouns, the way in which, in *Roland Barthes*, the first- and third-person singular and the initials R. B. are used simultaneously, sometimes even within the same fragment. Or the voice of others may be absorbed in order to be resuscitated later on by the voice of the writer, as in the case of Michelet.

To be against language means to recuperate theater not as expressiveness, but as a choreography of the body, as melody. Since the art of melody is dead, suggests Barthes in

The Pleasure of the Text, cinema can today give an idea of vocal writing. Cinematographic technology can capture the sound of speech from close by. It lets us see the full materiality of the mouth. It succeeds "in shifting the signified a great distance and in throwing, so to speak, the anonymous body of the actor into my ear."[51] Here lies the paradoxical role of technology: it must render the body in its materiality. Technology comes to resemble Michelet's vocal history. Both can use absence and death to report life, the vital quality of being, of reality. Anonymity—that anonymity of the actor's body that Barthes speaks of—does not imply abstract generality, but, on the contrary, a greater opportunity to experience particularity, contingency in its concreteness, the moment in its brief but euphoric temporal density. The thin temporality of our present was tragic in the first Barthes; it is joy in the years of *The Pleasure of the Text;* it will reappear as painfully nostalgic in *Camera Lucida,* when Barthes experiences the loss of the loved ones and analyzes the desperate link between time and death.

Voice is against language, which, in spite of the orality which linguistics attributes to it, does not have a grain, a weave, a tone, and, in its abstractness and generality, is lacking in singularity, in the very particularity of the person, of the body, of the timbre. The voice resembles a photographic image—which is another product of technology—since it is a particular existential episode which can only be repeated through technological reproduction. It is the fleeting moment, like pleasure, between being and nonbeing, and it has the extreme fragility of the body which perishes and dies. And when one hears a voice which immediately evaporates, capturing the moment in its elusiveness and pushing it into the past, one can only think—the way Barthes did when looking at a photograph of his dead mother, in *Camera Lucida,* the way anyone does when faced with a photograph—*ça a été:* the thing has been, it existed, and technology tries to capture it, but the thing will never repeat itself, never happen again. Voice and photography imply both presence and absence, and thereby indicate that reality exists, or even better, that it has existed, because what is concrete is also ephemeral, like pleasure, and will either be taken away by time, leaving behind a great void, or is fixed, like the objects seen by Hofmannsthal's traveler, in a reality that is both opaque and empty of meaning, and consequently unreal. On the other hand, that which is concrete can also be representation, and find its reality in the subtle space of the image, the paper of the photograph, the written page, in which writing—in spite of the whole grammatological epic of the French avant-garde—does *represent*, does transcribe voice and body, the way Barthes's pages on pleasure do, the way Michelet's history does.

As I have already recalled at the beginning of this chapter, Derrida identified the voice as the major proof of truth in western thought based, since Plato, on the centrality of *logos*. The voice has always been linked to presence, while writing has been confined to the mere role of recording the voice. Derrida's *Of Grammatology* proposes a deep questioning of the main structures of voice and presence, while indicating the primary importance of what voice and presence repressed: writing, which is absence, which is trace prior to any presence. Barthes, in spite of his insistence on writing, does not fully belong to this trend of thought. He is situated apart, neither in the "logocentric" stream, nor in the grammatological reversal of *logos*. Barthes does not fight for a theory, or a system of notions. This was true already with *Writing Degree Zero* and *Michelet*, before the time of *Roland Barthes*, before what Lavers calls the "theoretical bankruptcy of so many systems," and mainly those of Marx, Sartre, and Saussure.[52] Roger believes that the so-called "last Barthes" does not look back to his own past, "because such a past has always accompanied his work," since his youth's writings on Greek tragedy.[53] The voice-*logos* of Derrida is abstract, undetermined, absolute; the historical and concrete forms it takes are the accidents of a unique force, of a general philosophical illusion. For Barthes, the voice is the voice of somebody—even if this person is of course not realistically determined, because strict realism is poor, depressing, nonartistic. Barthes follows images, small and concrete episodes which, not unlike some events in *A la recherche du temps perdu*, are small but dense with emotions. He studies in detail the image onto which his mind stumbles, he stubbornly analyzes it, as through a magnifying glass. The all of *Writing Degree Zero* translates into intellectual terms the very concrete image of the writer alone in front of the white sheet of paper, in the same way *Camera Lucida* studies the effect of photography in general through the very concrete picture of Barthes's mother as a child. A concrete event, a particular image are for Barthes the occasions to speculate, to discuss in general terms. Even if he is and has been considered a theorist, his analyses often start from a very small and concrete detail: a scene, an image, a recollection. It would be enough to cite some fragments of *Roland Barthes*, especially those called "anamneses," or some passages from *Incidents*, to see Barthes's taste for calligraphic descriptions mixed with memories. He can recall the taste of "cold milk with sugar in it,"[54] or a restaurant in Rabat, or the stained pullover of "a certain Ahmed, nearby the train station."[55] The taste for details is at the basis of what I would call Barthes's *petite écriture artiste*, and of his pleasure for the *journal intime*, in the line of Gide: "Gide is my original language, my *Ursuppe*, my literary soup."[56]

Barthes did not really change the subjects of his investigation, as suggested by Lavers[57]: if the sorrows of love, childhood, or scenes of provincial life seem to be more intimate and bourgeois subjects than the writer's anguish or Michelet's headaches, Barthes's mode of investigation is seemingly based on what can be called a magnifying analysis, which patiently organizes all the elements of an experience, or a phenomenon, using terminologies which come

from different systems, like Marxism, Saussurian linguistics, or psychoanalysis. Therefore, Barthes does not
consider the pleasure of the text a philosophic argument
for a whole deconstruction of western metaphysics; for him
it is more important to indicate that undefinable feeling for
the anonymous body of the actor, for the moments of deep
pleasure in reading, for the attempt to catch the ephemeral
consistency of human voice. The voice for Barthes, as for
Michelet, does not correspond to the fullness of presence,
but to the trace of the body, to the mystery of its presence,
the disquieting sign of a lost reality, which we lose at the
very moment we try to represent it. Derrida conceives the
trace—which corresponds to writing, or to the signifier—
as a repressed force, in a timeless ontological purity, similar to the word in Mallarmé; and time, or history, is nothing but the manifold accumulation of the denials of such a
force. For Barthes the trace is the concrete image of something that happened, and carries the effect of time, which
passes and devours real things and real people. The image is
the little bit of body which is left to us after an event has
gone away and does not exist any longer. The reality which
evaporates can be the human voice, or the feast of pleasure,
or the whole presence of a person. The image gives back to
us a pale representation of that reality, and corresponds to
our impossible effort to retain things, people, events. As I
will argue in my third chapter, representation exorcises the
loss of life. Barthes finds himself more in the position of
Baudelaire contemplating the ephemeral vision of the passerby in the poem *A une passante*, than in the position of
Derrida criticizing the metaphysics of *phoné*, the whole
concept of representation. Barthes does not focus on the
ideological side of representation, but he perceives its sensual character, its nostalgic essence. For this reason, in *The
Pleasure of the Text*, he distinguishes between *figuration*
and *representation*. Figuration is "the way in which the
erotic body appears (to whatever degree and in whatever
form it may be) in the profile of the text," while representa-

tion is "*embarrassed figuration*, encumbered with other meanings than that of desire."[58] But we could simply speak of a good representation and a bad one, the good one being capable of moving us, making us wish, long for something, somebody.

Therefore we witness something quite disconcerting: the semiologist of Marxist origins, who had analyzed objects in order to rid them of the incrustations of meaning imposed by history and by the alienating power of language, finds himself facing a mute reality. He begins to want to make it speak, to take hold of it with a terminology which—although it is uncertain, precarious, reversible like the pair pleasure/bliss—is nevertheless a fragment of discourse, and not a blubbering text, a text which "might be said to *prattle*," in the choppy language of an infant, the prototype of a text which Barthes cannot tolerate.[59] Barthes is moved here by something like nostalgia, the nostalgia of the mythologist that Genette dwelled upon. He is moved to regret the disappearance of wooden toys, "an ideal material by virtue of its solidity and softness, the natural heat that it offers to the touch."[60] His nostalgia for the past, for things that are no more, is immense. Faced with loss, there is no other way to revive the body than to *name*, in order to make that which can no longer speak exist again—which is exactly what Michelet tried to do with his history, what the writer of the novel does.

Fatigue

And I was overwhelmed from imposing on my agonizing existence the superhuman burdens of life.—Marcel Proust

"All this should be considered as though it had been said by a character in a novel": this sentence is written on the inside of the front cover of *Roland Barthes*, a text which belongs to an undefined genre. Barthes produced it after having spoken at great length on the plurality of the text and the happy cohabitation of languages. His work has an internal coherence whereby thoughts and basic themes re-emerge or explode in a particular form, the fragment. Such a form results from the contamination of the maxim and the aphorism. The maxim belongs to the French tradition: La Rochefoucauld is one example, and, in 1961, Barthes wrote a foreword to his *Réflexions ou sentences et maximes*. The aphorism is Nietzsche's form whose influence was so visible in *The Pleasure of the Text*; the aphorism is also the form of Baudelaire's reflections, as in *Mon Coeur mis à nu* and *Fusées*. But one of Barthes's fundamental ideas, an idea which led to the meditations in *Writing Degree Zero*, maintains that modern writing succeeds in fusing the poetic or novelistic genre with the critical: such is the state of the great literary experiences of modernity from Mallarmé to Proust, Joyce, and Musil. What could have been more interesting for Barthes than the opportunity to write a critical text on his own work for the same collection of the Éditions du Seuil for which he had written *Michelet*? It was the perfect opportunity to stage in a fragmentary form a critical autobiography, one which would bring together personal photographs and figures of language and thought. In such a work the ego of the critic, would recognize, then lose, itself in a game of images, a Nietzschean masquerade, in discourse and ironic defenses, in a writing where all ideologies explode, including Marxist, Freudio-Lacanian, and avant-garde ones (in the genre of *Tel Quel*).

In *Roland Barthes* the terms "style" and "writing" finally coincide with each other. This occurs at the exact moment when Barthes is tired of semiology, of the Text, of the Lacanian orthodoxy, of all Parisian intellectual phenomena. It is the moment of the "vague torment of a *recession* toward the minor thing, the old thing he is when 'left to himself.' "[61] It is, then, the moment of a return to the body as it exists outside of all languages and systems, an anarchic moment, enclosed in that secret of the writer's body, style, which Barthes spoke of in *Writing Degree Zero*. Such an antisocial, silent secret, enclosed in the body of the writer, resembles the neutrality of matter, the neuter or neutral that Blanchot spoke of: "The neuter in the singular form names something that escapes naming . . . We call it simply and inconsiderately the thing. The thing, because . . . things are what is most familiar to us, since we live in an environment of things, although they are not transparent."[62] The neuter is a form excluded by language—or, at least, some languages—and indicates the thing, the very materiality of the thing. Even pleasure has something *neutral* about it. It escapes the mythologies of the right which uphold pleasure against intellectuality, and the mythologies of the left which consider pleasure an idea of the right that is to be suspected of hedonism, an idea upheld by people who are neither committed nor militant. Pleasure is "a drift, something both revolutionary and asocial, and it cannot be taken over by any collectivity, any mentality, any idiolect. Something *neuter?*"[63]

It is not my intention to propose a chronology whereby an existentialist Barthes of the 1950s was followed by a second Barthes, who was a semiologist until 1975, when *Roland Barthes* was published, and then by a third, the writer, after 1975. I only wish to highlight the gesture by which Barthes rejected all systems and returned to his own past writing, which included not only works and themes of the past, but also his own personal experience as a writer. The essence of the writing that came beforehand can be found in his conception of style as body, which he set forth in *Writing Degree Zero*. The past of the person resides in memories.

In *A Lover's Discourse: Fragments* Barthes wrote, in parentheses: "(In no love story I have ever read is a character ever *tired*. I had to wait for Blanchot for someone to tell me about Fatigue.)."[64] Paradoxically one gets tired of that which one loves, of love itself, of language. Fatigue is the specter of desire: one tires of what is desired and one tires of desiring. Language, like love, vacillates between the excitement of desire and fatigue. The tangible form of language fatigue is the stereotype, which in *Roland Barthes* is defined as that which *begins* to tire—the antidote, already announced in *Writing Degree Zero*, is the freshness of language.

Barthes is tired of those strong systems, Marxism and psychoanalysis. The expression "bourgeois ideology" struck him, for example in *Roland Barthes*, as having aged exceedingly. Time and usage erode words and concepts by fixing them in troublesome images. These images repeat themselves and make us feel obliged to repeat them. "The Image," according to the title of an article written in 1977, can be defined as Barthes's nausea: he finds himself face to face with language and conceptual stereotypes, and he experiences the horror of stupidity: "Consider the 'complete systems' (Marxism, Psychoanalysis), *initially* they have an (effective) function of counter-Stupidity: to pass through them is to educate oneself . . . But subsequently these systems themselves become stupid. Once they 'take,' there is stupidity. That is why it is inescapable. One feels like going elsewhere: *Ciao! No, thanks!*"[65] One should realize that this is not a condemnation of systems *qua* systems, but of the use of such systems, or rather, of their nonuse. The disgusting phenomenon for Barthes is the reification of systems in ordered words, in little dogmas. This phenomenon is the intellectual parasitism which makes one *stick* to discourse: Barthes speaks of the intimidations of language, of the clinging languages which stick to people—by virtue of which the militant is a parasite who is content with a certain discourse, with a number of stereotypes. One could easily accuse Barthes of being reactionary; one should, instead, remember that such an attitude pushes one toward a continual exercise of the intelligence. It can keep us from settling into given discourse, it can encourage us to change and be on a constant lookout for the erosion of forms and meaning. Instead of dwelling on Barthes's continual conversions or on his possible betrayal of semiology, one should insist on the basic loyalty of his thinking. To change means to be faithful: "For example, in the case of Semiology, which I helped constitute, I have been my own corrupter, I have gone over to the side of the Corrupters."[66] There was, above all, the idea that time corrodes words and that one has to liberate language from the incrustations of time. From this followed the idea that, since the pleasure of the text is the result of the cohabitation of various languages (the Text is seen as a happy Babel), the subject has to pass through a multiplicity of languages—true Nietzschean masks. Then there was the idea that the privileged moment of language lay in literature, especially in the novel, because the novel is the place in which stereotyped discourse and commonplaces are staged. It is as though one were to put quotation marks around "bourgeois ideology" or "denial" or some other word or phrase which has been excessively charged with meaning, which is, for that reason, empty: in the novel, Barthes tells us, the characters themselves function as quotation marks. The comparison is important because it explains his attraction to the novel that he demonstrated in his last works.

At the moment of fatigue, Barthes, the critic, encountered the very fatality of the essay—the usual form of his works—when compared with the novel. The essay is "doomed to *authenticity*—to the preclusion of quotation marks,"[67] that is, it is destined to adhere to language, and can use neither irony nor masks. From that moment, which has already been announced by the "character in a novel" that Barthes would like to be, one can glimpse a tension regarding the form of the novel. It is almost as though the abstract and totalizing idea of writing were to become perceptible not only in the practice of sentences, but also in the composition and construction of these sentences in a novel.

To pass from a suggestive and lyrical critical essay to a real and true novel—such is the project of one who had begun his career as a critic by asking himself questions about the status of literature. *To make* literature: such seems to be, in the 1980s, the answer of one who has witnessed the birth and dissolution of various theories. Barthes never wrote a novel, but he announced his need and intention to do so beginning in 1978. In any case, literature emerged as the ultimate value, especially in the literary form that was the most typical product of the nineteenth century, the novel. One cannot say, of course, that literature had always been of primary importance to Barthes, for example, when he was most concerned with constituting a method and founding semiology. But his passion for the sign was certainly a new way for him to love literature. As Roger wrote, Barthes has been "all his life the lucid and crazy lover of Literature."[68] As Genette had already remarked in the article quoted earlier, literature had always been at the core of Barthes's semiological research, because literature, as any signifying activity, makes use of signs. It entails, however, a proliferation of meaning, or what Barthes calls "the kitchen of meaning";[69] it deludes meaning, that is, it proposes it and suspends it. Literature is ambiguous: though it is made of language, it perverts the communicative nature of language itself by blocking its transitivity and making it, as Genette suggested, a site of uncertainty, of interrogation. In short, literature for Barthes, as for Lord Chandos, is a rhetoric of silence—such is the elegant oxymoron Genette used to indicate the dual character of literature. The essay, on the other hand, is a form of writing which stands in opposition to this silence: whether it communicates positive or negative values is of little importance. In an essay ideas are dense: they become consistent. The pact with time is brief; it wears through rapidly, revealing more than the philosophical systems relevant to it. It also exposes the ideology (or counterideology) which underwrites it. Now, more than ever, the critical essay is a form of writing destined to be dated as much by its content as by its jargon. Such is the curious condition of the critic. His language is burned by history, whereas the novel seems to profit from history as though it were an ornament. The essay, doomed to authenticity, is imprisoned in history, in the cultural structures of the historical period in which it has been written; the novel displays historical features as an embellishment, or dramatizes history, uses it as *maquillage*.

Literature is a "semantic evasion," Genette maintained, and "gives breath to the world, liberating it from the pressure of the social, which is a named meaning, and therefore a dead meaning."[70] In this case all the drama of Barthes's situation and that of the writer resides in the space which separates the statement "there is no meaning that is not named" from the vision of literature as "Orpheus who returns from hell": "One could say that literature is Orpheus returning from the underworld; as long as literature walks ahead, aware that it is leading someone, the reality behind it which it is gradually leading out of the unnamed—that reality breathes, walks, lives, heads toward the light of a meaning; but once literature turns around to look at what it loves, all that is left is a named meaning, which is a dead meaning."[71]

Orpheus

On language and writing, taken as magical operations, evocative witchcraft.—Charles Baudelaire

Orpheus's condition is perhaps the mental state in which Barthes most resembles Blanchot. The latter has captured all the ambiguity in the glance of that mythic figure: "When Orpheus descends to Eurydice, art is the power that causes the night to open. Because of the power of art, the night welcomes him; it becomes the welcoming intimacy, the understanding and the harmony of the first night. But Orpheus has gone down to Eurydice: for him, Eurydice is the limit of what art can attain; concealed behind a name and covered by a veil, she is the profoundly dark point towards which art, desire, death and the night all seem to lead."[72] The work of Orpheus does not consist, for Blanchot, in his securing an extreme point which the work reaches in its descent to the deep. It consists in bringing "it back into daylight" and, in daylight, giving it "form, figure, and reality."[73] And the inevitable law—the one which determines the impossibility of literature—is that Orpheus cannot not turn backward: "Orpheus has actually been turned towards Eurydice all along."[74]

But the difference between Blanchot and Barthes, between their very close visions of the writer's solitude, resides in the fact that, in the end, a critical essay is something different from literature, though it may be composed of language, like literature. Barthes remains a writer of essays, though the essay exploded in his hands, especially in *Roland Barthes*, *The Pleasure of the Text*, and *A Lover's Discourse*, all three of which recall the French—and rationalist—tradition of maxims and reflections. Talking about the maxim in *Roland Barthes*, he finds that "an aphoristic tone hangs about" his book and that the maxim is a "sort of *sentence-name*" and "is linked to classical ideology."[75] Barthes saw the novel as an ideal, the ideal form, and the ideal state of mind to which his work was aiming at last. He saw the form of the novel as a conversion, what he called in his 1978 lecture at the Collège de France "Longtemps, je me suis couché de bonne heure," his new life, *Vita Nuova*, which he was never able to attain. *Incidents*, published after his death, in 1987, is not a novel Barthes kept in his drawer, but, as I have already said, a *journal intime*, a collection of fragments in the same tone of the fragments of the anamneses in *Roland Barthes*, or of "Deliberation," published in *Tel Quel* in 1979 (and now in *The Rustle of Language*). As he wrote in his critical autobiography, while discussing his taste for fragments: "I proceed by addition, not by sketch; I have the antecedent (initial) taste for the detail, the fragment, the *rush*, and the incapacity to lead it towards a 'composition.' "[76] Meanwhile, Blanchot, an author of both essays and novels, leaned toward a precise system of thought, almost a philosophy or a mystique of passivity, of inspiration at the limits of madness. The most influential tradition for Blanchot is above all German (Hölderlin and Heidegger) and Jewish (especially Kafka, and the philosophy of Emmanuel Levinas). Blanchot understands the artistic work as synonymous with a violent and complete entry into poetry and the poetic essence of poetry: he quotes Rilke talking about a danger inherent in the work of art and believes that "the poet belongs to the poem." Writing means to risk, and "the work of art is linked to a risk, it is the affirmation of an extreme experience."[77] The artistic work can only make the artist "mad": Michelangelo became progressively more tormented, Goya more possessed, and Nerval gloomy. Hölderlin died to the reasonable possession of himself,[78] and Nietzsche slid into madness. For Blanchot there is something even more important than the work of art, a greater gift, and that is the loss of the work itself: "The work is everything for Orpheus, everything except that desired gaze in which the work is lost, so that it is also only in this gaze that the work can go beyond itself, unite with its origin and establish itself in impossibility."[79] In short, Blanchot searches, through literature, an idea of the void, of total absence, of infinity, of nonrepresentable eternity. "To write is to surrender oneself to the fascination of the absence of time . . . The time of the absence of time is without a present, without a presence. This 'without a present,' however, does not refer to a past."[80] Blanchot suggests that literature is silence and cannot be reduced to language, whereas Barthes is more *realistic*, more classical, more a humanist than a mystic. Barthes is, certainly, terrified of fullness, which is for him "a bad form"; it is repetition and stereotype, reassuring ideology, but in "Digressions" he warns us against conceiving of the void "in the form of an absence (of the body, of things, of emotions, words, etc.: *nothingness*)."[81] The work of writing that he is thinking about "consists neither in the amelioration of communication, nor in its destruction, but in the *filigreeing* of it: that is more or less (parsimoniously) what has made classical writing."[82] Without trying to subvert linguistic signs, or breaking syntax, one should try today to wear "the mask of the legible, to parody it, or rather, to simulate it."[83] And the *simulacrum*, the image, can be positive, pleasing, and give pleasure, because it is beautiful, beautiful *to me*, and not because it is accepted by society or fashion. Barthes is completely on the side of the corporeal, whereas Blanchot is attracted to the incorporeal—we will see how, for Barthes, the lack of a body is the ultimate suffering and knowledge of suffering.

For Blanchot art is "terribly serious" and "not allowed to mislead."[84] For Barthes, on the other hand, art is the Baudelairean game of hypocrisy and simulation: this is the full and dazzling meaning of fiction—which does not rule out tragedy, but treats it ironically, lessening its weight. Barthes's ultimate proposition was fiction, the novel, or fragments in prose—which, in spite of their disconnected images, remain coherent like poems in prose. His desire for the novel, as Roger pointed out, is at the edge of hysteria, of imagining very intensely something which does not exist.[85] Blanchot, on the other hand, proposes poetry—even if the distinctions between prose and poetry are fluid. The highest human experience is poetry, the poetic word being an errancy without any rest, exactly like the prophetic word, as Blanchot reads it.[86] I would say that Barthes has a hedonistic side in his appreciation of literature and art, while hedonism is completely foreign to Blanchot, who condemned it, as when he talked about "the petty happiness of aesthetic pleasure."[87] Of course Barthes and Blanchot have much in common, and Barthes himself, in his last years, in the years of his obsession with the novel, spoke of a vocation and a prophecy. Between the two French writers there is a difference of experience similar to the one Blanchot saw between Mallarmé and Rilke, who are so close in their understanding of poetry. Both of them perceive poetry as related to absence and death. But Blanchot finds between the two what I would call a difference in coloristic temperament. Rilke never ceases "to fall towards the center in a silent, immobile, endless fall," while Mallarmé annihilates and suspends beings "into the dazzling vivacity of the instant," in its sudden flash which makes absence visible as if it were "pure presence."[88] In other words, Rilke celebrates the invisible, while Mallarmé makes the invisible visible, just for an instant—an instant of body, a cruel illumination.

The haiku, a fragmentary form that Barthes had favored, from the time of his Japanese experience of *L'Empire des signes*, is legible; it has the sudden light of the instant. It resembles the poem in prose, a detached and intense, yet visible, image—what else are the figures of a lover's discourse, if not images? According to Blanchot literature participates deeply in the invisible, it tends vertiginously toward the invisible, toward that which Orpheus cannot look at face to face but nonetheless desires to see. For Barthes literature participates in the visible and tangible. As he said in *Roland Barthes*, his illness consists in *seeing* language as a real body, the first and last foundation of literature. In fact, the deep desire of one who is fascinated by haiku becomes the good literary message according to the classical code: clarity, elegance, simplicity, grace. Haiku is a nonsign, a fragment of nonsense, a total loss of meaning. It is the sign displayed as spectacle, as picture, as image, and therefore rich in its simplicity and suggestive (or *tremblé*, shaking and shaken, as Genette says). For there are two types of image for Barthes, the good and the bad. The bad image is that which takes us back to society, that which fixes and recognizes us: the stereotype. The good image is that which appears as figure, or rather as a series of figures.

The imaginary (*l'imaginaire*) is a magic word for Barthes. It is filled with personal and cultural memories: images of childhood and youth, like the photographs in *Roland Barthes*, the imaginary as it is found in Sartre, Bachelard, Lacan, in which forms move like waves—the forms of the body and the self, phrases that are read, desired, written, and the reality of lived existences. The imaginary is a negative value when it implies fixed attachment to an image. It is a positive value when it is the domain of images that come and go, like figures in a dance, in a changing choreography. One should not, therefore, expect Barthes to be loyal to the Lacanian imaginary, although he often refers to it. He always slightly disfigures Lacan's notions, even in *S/Z*. He inserts them in his intellectual research like figures in a tapestry, like the figures described in James's short story, "The Figure in the Carpet," a literary secret that is both obvious and elusive, a secret that it would be foolish to try to identify or isolate once and for all.

Barthes was, of course, fascinated by the link between the ego and the image. The moment par excellence of the imaginary in Lacan is "the mirror stage": the infant, long before the identification of the ego in language, long before the use of language, is able to recognize its image in the mirror as an image.[89] (On the other hand, when an animal sees its image in a mirror, it thinks it is seeing another member of its species.) Man, therefore, knows from the first months of life the pleasure of fiction and of imaginary doubling. Even though the infant cannot speak, cannot say "I," it is already taken by the symbolic order of language, because its recognition of itself in the mirror indicates its future capacity to identify itself fictitiously with the linguistic "I." But Barthes does not want to confirm an orthodoxy, to follow the Lacanian mathemes and concepts; however unsystematic, they form an institutional science, psychoanalysis.

Acting like a good phenomenologist of Sartrean origin, Barthes measures everything against himself, that is to say, against his own writing, and he gives the same cognitive value to mental objects, or theoretical concepts, and to physical objects, or the forms of reality. Above all, with regard to the imaginary, he puts himself in the position of Baudelaire, and could himself have said this sentence, which appears in *Mon Coeur mis à nu:* "Glorifying the cult of images (my great, only, primitive passion)." Barthes was not looking for the symbolic side of images, as Blanchot does, but for their visual richness and phantasmagoria, as if they were musical variations. Thus, when it came to language, the symbolic order par excellence, Barthes never looked for its basic, omnipresent structure—which would have put him in a Kafkaesque position or would have suggested to him fragments like those in Blanchot's *La Part du feu*, in which words are turned back on themselves and rolled up in their own meaning or etymology. On the contrary, he has always looked for images—wearisome or pleasing, fresh or stereotyped—a festival of words, a theater of figures. It is a matter of verbal images, of myth, and of poetry as Vico understood it, of Michelet's myth as Barthes defined it in his article on Michelet, "Michelet, l'histoire et la mort": a tension between categories and the body, between a Science and a Poetry, that is, between the abstract and the concrete.

Barthes grew tired of Lacan's emphasis on the body and desire as caught, both, in the symbolic order of language— or in the interplay between the imaginary and the symbolic in which the symbolic wins out. He looked for something else, the *démodé*, the lover's discourse, the *pietas* for the dead mother, the body in its indomitable, almost brutal expression: "Once the exaltation has lapsed, I am reduced to the simplest philosophy: that of endurance (the natural dimension of real fatigue)."[90]

The restrictions and obligations of a school are intolerable, like those of love or of social images which assault us and stick to our skin, trapping us in given behavior, in definitions, and in meanings. Only one wish remains: to be silent. Silence would then be the only answer to the heaviness and imposture of the stereotype. But aren't silence and literature the same thing? In the preface to his *Critical Essays*, Barthes maintained: "Writing must go hand in hand with silence; to write is in a sense to become 'still as death,' to become someone to whom the *last word* is denied; to write is to offer others, from the start, that last word."[91] And this other is more than ever the language of others, a language that is a stereotype, a way of fixing the world in codes and definitions. What can be more conformist than language, which rules human exchange?[92] On the other hand, only language can free us from stereotypes. It is both extremely poor and extremely rich, and forces us to travel its length and breadth, as though we were dancing figures on an infinite stage of words and sentences.

The antidote to stereotypes, to the stereotypes of today, can be found in silence, or in the *démodé*. One must wander through the past, become a *flâneur* of obsolete forms that are no longer in fashion, that have preserved the imprint of an era in which they had the value of a signified (and were consequently stereotypes). When these forms are taken up again, they appear flattened, like images— and images are a flattening of the real, they are the light and slightly tangible form of the real, in the same way that voice is the shadow of a presence, that a song is fleeting— regarding the singer Panzera, who belonged to another musical generation and stopped singing just before the advent of the long-playing record, Barthes said that "it is the perishable which glistens so heartbreakingly in this singing."[93]

Barthes had already commented on the theme of regret in Bataille and Nietzsche: "A certain form of the present is disparaged, a certain form of the past is exalted; neither this present nor this past is actually historical; they are both read according to the formal, ambiguous movement of *decadence*. Thus is born the possibility of non-reactionary regret, or a *progressive* regret. *Decadence* is not read, contrary to the word's accepted connotation, as a sophisticated, hypercultural condition, but, on the contrary, as a *deflation of values*."[94] As a sophisticated, hypercultural condition, decadence is for Barthes a leveling in the positive sense, in contrast to the loss and flattening of values dictated by society and seen as negative.

Suddenly, as Barthes said in the fragment of his diary published in *Tel Quel* in 1979, he stopped caring about being modern. He did not care if semiology, or his semiology in particular, was neither modern nor scientific, whether it entered into the decadent, apocalyptic history of values which flatten into images. It is a loss for the meaning of images, for the language of that which consists—the stereotype—but it is a flattening, an art of capturing "that which can die" for the logic of decadence. And one can experience in this loss the sad and extenuated pleasure of the real, of the past as image, flattened out the way, in a photograph, the body is flattened into a semblance of being. And though photography is an art that has earned little recognition, though it is too young to have given rise to any developed aesthetic theory, it is an art which gives an undeniable certainty: the image we see *was real*, it really existed in the past. Photography cannot be separated from a taste for decay, decadence, because it is the art of capturing not only that which can die, but also that which is already dead, in order to restore it like a shadow. Barthes's strong taste for photography was not a semiological fascination, even though the study of photography allows one to understand how messages circulate. The taste for this art is a tearing passion for transient things. It is a taste for the *démodé* but also a classical, ancient taste, ancient like human suffering, like the suffering that Ulysses knew when, in hell, he tried in vain to embrace the shadow of his dead mother.

And so, in the world of the present where there is so little room for literature, we reach the point, *démodé* and decadent, when it is time to go toward literature. Barthes's cruel paradox is that the semiology which he embodied at the Collège de France is not a winning discipline, the discipline of the future, of computer science, but the form of loss, of regret, of decadence: "Literary semiology is, as it were, that journey which lands us in a country free by default; angels and dragons are no longer there to defend it. Our gaze can fall, not without perversity, upon certain old and lovely things, whose signified is abstract, out of date. It is a moment at once decadent and prophetic, a moment of gentle apocalypse, a historical moment of the greatest possible pleasure."[95]

To continue to write means to endure; endurance means

for Barthes the execution of a tremendous, infinite task, a labor of Sisyphus requiring enormous effort: to climb and descend to infinity, to conduct writing to the other side of literary semiology and even of literature. To continue to write means to move toward a mute and opaque thing, a thing without language, outside every language, to go toward the real (reality), the impossibility literature has been searching for forever. The paradox is nevertheless that the writer wants to write, and turn reality into more reality; literature transforms reality into more reality, into a deeper reality. Of course, this literature is not realistic; it is not the literature of description that Proust considered an art "without beauty, a mere vain and tedious duplication of what our eyes see and our intellect records."[96]

Barthes succeeds in developing the brutal reality of death into the deep reality of literature, because a writer, in Proust's words, is not like "most men" who do not, nor will ever, see their real life, "because they do not seek to shed light upon it." To shed light: this is the question in *Camera Lucida*, as the French title announces with the pun "*chambre claire*." Those who write want to escape the danger of forgetting their real life. They do not let their past be, as Proust remarked, "like a photographic dark-room encumbered with innumerable negatives which remain useless because the intellect has not developed them."[97]

For the last Barthes, Proust represents a vocation, a revelation. Numerous connections can be found between them. We will now return to certain positions of Barthes in the 1950s and 1960s, namely, on literary realism and the use of the first person. The shifting from one statement to another, and the pronouncements in "Inaugural Lecture," will help us to give perspective to Barthes's interest in Proust and the form of the essay. We will finally see how the third paradox comes about: in *Camera Lucida*, a most open Proustian text, Michelet reemerges from Barthes's past as the figure of his obsession with history, death, and the *démodé*.

Les raisons qui me poussent à écrire sont multiples, et les plus importantes sont, il me semble, les plus secrètes. Celle-ci peut-être surtout: mettre quelque chose à l'abri de la mort.—André Gide, *Journal*

The Real

To be simply true, to be what things themselves are, to be nothing more than they are, to be nothing if not through them, like them, as much as they.—Adolphe Thiers

We arrive now at the most difficult point of the Barthesian enterprise, the breaking point for his modern sensibility, the point beyond which no philosophy can go. Between words and things, between reality and language lies the abyss seen by Hofmannsthal, an abyss which can only be bridged painfully by modernity. Literature is in a privileged position, or in a damned one, relative to this abyss.

Barthes's voyage moves from one statement to another which seems contradictory, but no sentence is guilty of logical contradiction in the changing patterns of literature, in its geography of words and images. Barthes wrote in "Literature and Signification" this passage already quoted: "Literature is Orpheus returning from the underworld; as long as literature walks ahead, aware that it is leading someone, the reality behind it . . . that reality breathes, walks, lives, heads toward the light of a meaning."[1] Then he states in "Inaugural Lecture" that "literature, whatever the school in whose name it declares itself, is absolutely, categorically *realist.*"[2] Barthes finally talks in *Camera Lucida* about the reality of sorrow: "All this under the instance of 'reality'— and no longer through the elaborations of the text, whether fictional or poetic, which itself is never credible *down to the root.*"[3]

The first stage of this voyage is tied to the Orphic situation of literature, discussed in the previous chapter, because of which the writer, like Orpheus, cannot turn back toward what he loves, for if he did, he would find himself holding a dead meaning in his hands, that is, a named meaning. This situation is paradoxical and once again goes against language, in spite of all the affirmations that literature is language, and in spite of the way structuralism privileges language, when it implies that reality is mute but that literature can make it speak, or that literature can breathe life into the world. On the other hand, the fact that if one were to turn toward this reality, one would find it completely named, filled with dead meaning, implies that reality resides entirely in language and can be nothing but this "false" language that has been used and abused to the point of banality.

Thus the silence and opacity of things are both literature's point of departure and its point of arrival, because literature tears its language not from silence but from dead meaning, from that which has been said and said all over again, named and renamed too often. Originality is the necessary condition that language requires in order to become literature and to avoid the (deadly) banality of the message and of language itself. Literature is a way of varying it, of forming combinations which differ from common ones. One can analyze several of Barthes's reflections on literary realism from the perspective of what can be called literary Orphism, since it reflects Orpheus's situation.

First of all there is the idea of a new historian of literature or of criticism. In an interview given in 1961 Barthes said that until now "realism has been defined much more by its content than by its technique."[4] He never questioned the idea that literature copies something. But we can call "reality" the physical world, or the social or the cultural one: in order to copy the real, one must necessarily choose one sphere over another. Realism, therefore, is a choice and the responsibility of a choice, Barthes maintained in a Sartrean vein. But—and here he was speaking as a structuralist—literature is nothing other than language, and language is a system of meaning before it becomes literature. Consequently if one says one sees something, one is, first of all, speaking and choosing to say: "I see a bed or I see a window or a color." One is actualizing operations of selection, categorization, and discontinuity, which are exactly those operations which constitute a linguistic message or chain of signification, for which the referent—the object—is not as important as the relationship between the different words that are used and the system composed by these words. Literature can be found in this relational play of words; it carries and develops it. It is therefore profoundly unreal because it moves even further away from the referent than normal language. Not only is it not an analogous copy of reality, but *on the contrary, it is the very consciousness of the unreality of language,*[5] as Barthes said in a provocative formula which sought to jeopardize every realistic myth. He challenged the conviction that language does nothing but represent reality, and that reality existed before language. One must instead realize that words create things by giving them their reality.

One could also express this idea by saying that the concept creates the thing. Lacan, speaking of the Freudian *fort-da*, defines words as a presence made of absence. For him the word comes into existence by being the very trace of a nothing; he maintains that it is "the world of words which created the world of things, which is at first confused in the *hic et nunc* of everything in the state of becoming."[6] Structuralism, at least in its early stages, turned realism on its head, excluding the referent—the object, reality, things—and privileging language or discourse—not meanings but the ways in which meanings are shaped. Thus Barthes, in the early sixties, greeted Foucault's *Madness and Civilization* enthusiastically because, like Saussure's linguistics, this history was not concerned with the referent, but excluded the idea of a natural relationship between words and things. It did not define madness as a substance, a nosographical reality, a medical fact, or as the object of a branch of knowledge whose history one must retrace. Madness is "*nothing but this knowledge itself:* madness is not a disease, it is a variable and perhaps heterogeneous *meaning*, according to the period; Foucault never treats madness except as a functional reality: for him it is the pure function of a couple formed by reason and unreason, observer and observed."[7] Madness is a knot of discourses founded on oppositions—the way Saussure's phonemes are a functional reality founded on oppositions.

While realism was being rejected and literature was being considered the consciousness of the unreality of language, but before the full explosion of structuralism, Barthes demonstrated a great interest in a few developments of contemporary literature, the so-called *Nouveau Roman* (which has been linked to the structuralist brand of *Nouvelle Critique*). Regarding Robbe-Grillet, Barthes spoke of objective literature, or of a new realism that would be capable of liquidating analogical illusion. In fact, in Robbe-Grillet's novels the object is described minutely, but not analogically, as it is in the realistic or naturalistic novel, in which every descriptive detail includes an implicit judgment, a moral or human value, and the object is extremely tactile, synesthetic, full of memories and suggestions. In the realistic novel, in the manner of Zola, the object is described in relation to man and to man's movement toward it; but in Robbe-Grillet's descriptions humanism falls away, leaving only space. The characteristic of the object is to be here, to be there, and not simply to be. The object is not something or other, it is there, and accosts us with its character as thing: it has nothing to do with symbols, correspondences, sensations, significations: "It is merely an optical resistance."[8] For Hofmannsthal's returning voyager, objects were also pure optical resistance, the obsessive presence of disjointed objects, in his hotel room or in the city streets, aggressive by virtue of their *being there*, in their invasion of space. Lord Chandos's *words* were also isolated, terrible, menacing, eyes that stared at him.

Barthes argues that the aggressive isolation of the object is part of a course, typical of modern art, which does violence to vision the way certain violently visual contemporary paintings or films do. The writing of objective literature is geometrical and superficial (on the surface), it aims "to assassinate the classical object."[9] It explores the object in all its dimensions without privileging any one of them: "It is therefore the opposite of poetic writing." In short, objective literature excludes the continual allusiveness of things and words, the old psychology of the subject, who moves through events and meanings. One could say that it is thanks to its radical objectivity that such literature avoids falling into Orpheus's position and ending up with dead meaning. It seeks to be the experience of pure, total space, outside of time and human subjectivity, outside, therefore, of the life and death of meaning. One could hint that Robbe-Grillet is completely against language, the halo of meaning, which is always present in language, however meaningless it sounds. Language, even the most broken language, condemns us to meaning. Robbe-Grillet would like words to be as precise as geometrical lines, as spatial edges, and, as I said, Barthes compares his technique both to the spatial violence of contemporary painting and to the cinema.

Robbe-Grillet's objectivity or literalness, which fascinated Barthes so much, is a kind of extreme phenomenological position, the outermost limit of existential literature, of the absurd, so extreme that one can no longer speak of the absurd, as Sartre and Camus did, because speaking of it would inevitably posit the absurd as a meaning. Such a literature offers a phenomenology of perception, completely focused on the object, which breaks off all intersubjective relationships, all analyses of the rapport between exterior and interior. Absolute exteriority is reached, space is the only dimension, and it is timeless: "The event is never *focused*."[10] Furthermore, Robbe-Grillet's objects are not natural, but technological: he is the novelist of the contemporary world—of the 1950s—where the novel "teaches how to look at the world no longer with the eyes of a confessor, a physician, or of God—all significant hypostases of the classical novelist—but with the eyes of a man walking in his city with no other horizon but the spectacle before him, no other power than that of his own eyes."[11] It is not by chance that one of Robbe-Grillet's most famous novels bears the title *Le Voyeur*. Blanchot wrote a short essay on this novel, insisting on the aspect of visibility, and what he called "the radiant presence of space."[12] Blanchot talks about the impassibility and cruelty of the staring eyes, of total vision. Hofmannsthal's traveler perceives with fear the presence of things, their visual violence; Mathias in *Le Voyeur* reaches a more radical position, which Blanchot defines as "closer to the mathematical precision of ideal description."[13] Here there is no fear, no terror, no interior analysis: just a shapeless and depthless space, a blinding clarity.

"Objective Literature" (1954) and "Literal Literature" (1955), the two essays that Barthes wrote on Robbe-Grillet in the 1950s, took the same direction: they focused on description, on the object, and commented on the silence of meaning. They opposed the new avant-gardist realism to the older, traditional realism. They were in some sense satisfied with the new, and did not pursue questions about literature, about the meaning of the world and of things, questions that can never be answered. Actually, the early Robbe-Grillet and Barthes, critic of Robbe-Grillet, believed that an answer was possible: there is no meaning, there are only objects. The modern world is the end of the tyranny of meaning. Blanchot went further: "Novelists can never be reminded too often that it is not they who write their books but they are only the medium through which these emerge and that, however clear-headed they intend to be, they are undergoing an experience which transcends them."[14] For this reason, because of this transcending force, Blanchot found that, beyond Robbe-Grillet's craftsmanship and his experimental mastery, the main achievement of his novels "is the clarity which pervades them, a clarity akin to the strange invisible light that gives to some of our important dreams their reality."[15] Blanchot perceived that *Le Voyeur* tries to abolish the meaning of what we call "inwardness," nevertheless its objective space resembles "our own private nightmare space." Perfect objectivity reaches the mystery of dreams. There are therefore two sides in Robbe-Grillet. In a later essay, written in 1962, Barthes distinguished between a Robbe-Grillet "thing-oriented" and the "humanist." Barthes would also talk of Robbe-Grillet's theoretical error, which "was merely to suppose that there is a *Dasein* of things, antecedent and exterior to the language, which he believed literature was obliged to rediscover in a final impulse of realism."[16] In spite of its technical originality, objective literature, which understood the opacity of things and of language, is not able to present itself as the consciousness of language's unreality. Robbe-Grillet doesn't seem to realize that language creates things, since language is meaning. No human gesture can exclude meaning, and from the very suspension of meaning a multiplicity of suppositions arise. Thus, the meaning that Robbe-Grillet sought to congeal in his geometrical forms comes back frantically. Critics and readers try endlessly to decipher *Last Year in Marienbad;* they ask themselves questions about its meaning, and cover its gardens, stuccoes, plumed overcoats with explanations. It is then that the Orphism, which seemed to have been excluded by the *Nouveau Roman,* reappears as the very nature of literature, caught between the life and death of meaning.

But the question of realism is not particular only to literature. Since the nineteenth century, it informs historical discourse, which, more than literary realism, is founded on the belief that the referent (the object or fact) is external to discourse, "though without its ever being possible to reach it outside this discourse."[17] It then becomes necessary to analyze the privileged position that reality holds in discourse. We can only demythologize the referential illusion by identifying it as the reality effect: "Historical discourse does not follow the real, it merely signifies it, constantly repeating *this happened,* without this assertion ever being anything but the signified *wrong side* of all historical narration."[18] In 1968 Barthes wrote that the analysis of the effect of the real should be able "to challenge in a radical fashion, the age-old aesthetic of 'representation.' "[19] His words were part of the epic of the 1960s, of a political and semiological hope: to liberate the sign. But the radical questioning of the sign should take the form of silence, the end of representation and of the sign itself. It should be the end of both the sign balanced in its relationship between signifier and signified and the unbalanced sign which leans toward the signifier, and corresponds to the new, modern, avant-garde conception of the sign. Exactly the way the history of madness could only be true if written by a madman: "But then it would not be written in terms of history, so that we are left with the incoercible bad faith of knowledge."[20] The fatality of every thought, of every discourse on discourse, of every metalanguage is that metalanguage is always terrorist, as Barthes wrote. This is a disturbing statement for those who realize how essential the logical distinction between language-object and meta-language is to modern language, for those who know how important it has been for modern literature, since Flaubert, to see itself as double, "at the same time object and scrutiny of that object, utterance and utterance of that utterance, literature-object and metaliterature about this word."[21]

Speech dirties one's hands: "This is an endless dialectic, which can seem sophistical only to minds possessed of a reason substantial as a nature or a right; the others will experience it dramatically, or generously, or stoically; in any case they know that bewilderment, that vertigo of discourse on which Michel Foucault has cast so much light, a vertigo which appears not only upon contact with madness, but indeed each time that man, taking his distances, observes the world as different, which is to say each time he writes."[22] Writing becomes the act of looking at the world as though it were not the world. But what else could it be, this thing so different from reality, if not language itself?

Barthes's article on Foucault dates back to 1961, but, in spite of the enthusiasm for the new history touched off by Foucault, his consciousness of the ambiguity of writing and of the abyss between reality and language is already close to his pessimistic "Inaugural Lecture" of 1978. The sentence previously quoted, "Literature, whatever the school in whose name it declares itself, is absolutely, categorically *realist*," seems the antithesis of the statement that "Literature is the consciousness of the unreality of language" only if one isolates this last sentence and does not read it alongside other statements Barthes made in the same period, when he was caught in the paradox of writing, in the oscillations of the consciousness of the writer. I did not, therefore, accept an immobilist reading of Barthes, according to which Barthes's thinking never changed, but I also reject a Hegelian reading. My solution is a paradoxical position that combines the two readings, according to the double register of identity and difference. Such is the inexplicable register of time which travels through our bodies showing us that they are always the same, but also always changing. One has the same experience when looking at photographs of oneself; it was Barthes's experience when he saw the photographs of his childhood: a disquieting combination of recognition and denial. This double reading enables one to distinguish in Barthes the symptoms of a crisis, or of fatigue, from the very beginning. Here again Barthes can be seen in the same position of Hofmannsthal: in his juvenile poems, which were signed with the pseudonym Loris, one can already detect the indecency of language and read the theme of silence which explodes in *Lord Chandos* later on.[23]

The realism characteristic of all literature, which Barthes discusses in "Inaugural Lecture," is literature's rush to speak the world, knowing that it is different from the world, because reality is a multidimensional order, whereas language is unidimensional. There are no parallels between the two orders, but we behave as though this were not the case, either because we believe, like Adolphe Thiers or historians in general, that language can reproduce reality (we then get caught up in the illusion of referentiality), or because, like Lacan, we define the real as the impossible, as that which escapes discourse. Men reject the abyss, the fundamental lack of correspondence between reality and language, and by their rejection found language and produce literature.

Literature, then, cannot be without the impulse to represent: "From ancient times to the efforts of our avant-garde, literature has been concerned to represent something. What? I will put it crudely: the real."[24] Barthes was no longer trying, in an avant-gardist gasp, to challenge the old aesthetic of representation, but, like a true classicist, he was seeking the eternal course of literature in its own power of representation. Like a modernist, he knew that reality is not totally representable and that "men ceaselessly try to represent it by words."[25] He had reached the point of fusion between classicism and modernism, or was following in the footsteps of Baudelaire, who founded modernity and the very need for the modern when, in *Le Peintre de la vie moderne*, he announced as a principle that all modernity should be worthy of being ancient.

Literature (or writing or text—at this point the definitions become unimportant) gathers together all forms of knowledge without fixing any of them, without making a fetish out of any of them. Literature lives off of indirect light—the light of various knowledges, the light of the real. Literature becomes the locus of prophecy and of incessant utopia, of a splendid *unreality:* a language that represents the real in a play of words that signifies it. But literature does not consolidate any message into stereotypes. The utopia is a language free from the gregarious character of speech, which is always the servant of some power.

Later we will explore this theme of language and power, but for now I wish to comment only on the way the terms "reality" and "unreality," relative to literature and language, reappear in "Inaugural Lecture" in a different perspective. In the interview in *Critical Essays*, the unreality of language, literature's awareness of itself as literature, was valuable as a polemic against literary realism and nosological realism, that is to say against tradition, and became the foundation of an absolute faith in the science of language. The unreality Barthes spoke of in his lecture at the Collège de France is linked to the fundamental realism of all literature which is founded on a real delirium, the lack of correspondence between reality and language; literature wishes to overcome the crude quality of common language. If there is any polemical spirit here, it is only a feeble shadow, a solitary soul's gesture of rejection directed against the avant-garde, against a semiology which has by this time become an academic institution, which has, willingly or not, compromised with power. To discuss in

1978 the realism of literature is not the same as proposing a return to tradition; instead, it understands tradition as embodied in all our revolts and perceives the *démodé* as a prophecy of decadence.

Barthes's prophecy resembles Nietzsche's and Bataille's: the risk of an impossible word, of a writing that would insult all stereotypes. Dancing with one's pen means going in all directions, even where one does not expect to go, it means turning a morality into a paradox, following the rhythm of the body in motion, in a tragic choreography.

But the Barthesian prophecy, which is directed toward the saving of literature in a world that no longer believes in it, cannot be read apart from a biographical episode that found its way into his writings. That was the death of his mother, which is the theme of *Camera Lucida*, Barthes's last book, published shortly before his own death in 1980. The novelistic character that Barthes spoke of in *Roland Barthes* returns here. Every character of a classical novel must measure itself against life, against passions. The desire for the classical novel with its characters presents a real paradox for the critic who himself had once attacked traditional biographical criticism and who had been fascinated by the radically objective literature of Robbe-Grillet, which was without traditional characters. But as Barthes said in a lecture at the Collège de France, "intellectual conversions are the very pulsion of the intelligence,"[26] and every researcher has a right and duty to change.

Furthermore, as Barthes said in "Inaugural Lecture," life is subtle and science is coarse; only literature is fit to represent life and the real in its multiple, infinite aspects.

The taste of reality and the inadequacy of words to represent it are experienced acutely at the painful moment of confrontation with death. Death is perhaps the only precise perception of reality that is given to us: death is the *res*, terrible and unspeakable, the true silence beyond all discourses on silence, beyond all metaphors of death—the death of literature, the death of art, the death of the author.

Metaphors of death contain only a little of death, whereas complete, true death, the one that is confronted when one looks in vain for loved ones who are dead, strikes like an impossible reality. Then Barthes, looking for his dead mother in *Camera Lucida*, could only write the sentence cited at the beginning of this chapter as the last step of his reflections on literature and reality: "All this under the instance of 'reality'—and no longer through the elaborations of the text, whether fictional or poetic, which itself is never credible *down to the root.*"

Abjuration

The noncredibility of the text originates in the language that constitutes it. The freedom one enjoys when speaking and writing is only provisional: language is always a prison, not only because the writer must struggle in order to find his form, to tear it from the wearing out of language, but also because, at the very moment he finds it, the institution will take possession of it, and turn it into what it wants: a science, a fashion, a motto, a stereotype.

If one is to continue writing, to adhere to a philosophy of forbearance, one must accept the responsibility of one's own work, even if it means abjuring, as Pasolini has said, as Barthes wrote in "Inaugural Lecture." To abjure does not mean to disclaim one's writing. Written texts, in any case, no longer belong to the writer once they have been published because the reader, and not the writer, has the last word. To abjure means to continue stubbornly to write, even though language in our liberal society is *fascist*, not in the sense that it prevents us from speaking, but in the sense that it forces us to speak: "But language—the performance of a language system—is neither reactionary nor progressive; it is quite simply fascist."[27] Barthes uttered these scandalous words at his inaugural lecture at the Collège de France, and thereby condemned semiology at the very moment it was being instituted as a discipline. Writing is against language, but from the moment that it is recognized publicly, it becomes language again, and it is recuperated as such.

"Inaugural Lecture" is Barthes's most desperate text. Susan Sontag contrasted Barthes's political lightness with Walter Benjamin's political awareness: "Barthes, who was not tormented by the catastrophes of modernity or tempted by its revolutionary illusions, had a post-tragic sensibility. He refers to the present literary era as 'a moment of gentle apocalypse.' Happy indeed the writer who can pronounce such a phrase."[28] I would say that the one who pronounced these words at the Collège de France was on the contrary an extremely sad, tired man, retired from life and the debates of modernity, after having tasted them all, a man who loved literature and asked himself if he could still be a writer, if he still had the time, the time to write the novel he desired. The sweet apocalypse of letting himself die is a languid and destructive death, as in a tragedy that is no longer a tragedy because it is bloodless and worn. The fact is that tragedy returns as farce, as Barthes said quoting Marx in *Roland Barthes:* "Intensely struck, that first time, and struck forever by that notion of Marx's that in History tragedy sometimes recurs, *but as farce* . . . Farce . . . is a metaphor which leans, fades, and falls (slackens)."[29] Written for a highly institutional event, "Inaugural Lecture" appeared at a time that was extremely ambiguous for the French intellectual of the left, for the avant-garde in general, and for all those who, in some way, believed in the opposition of 1968. It was the moment of an encounter between the spirit of rebellion and the recognition by the great institutions of the state, a recognition that was both desired and rejected (this situation had already been experienced by Baudelaire—the case was analyzed by Sartre— who failed in his own repeated attempts to join the Académie française). Where does one place oneself after one's work has been accepted and consecrated by the institutions? How can one manage to remain truly outside power?

It is not enough to say, as Barthes did, that "honor is usually a diminution of power." It is not enough to tell oneself that fortunately the Collège de France is an institution without students, an institution enabling the professor not to enslave himself to a direct knowledge. A professor there is not in a position in which he must judge, choose, or promote. He is free to pursue the sole activities of research and lecturing on his own research, "to dream his research aloud."[30] All this is not enough: so then, who is the guilty party? Language, the *logos*, discourse, any act of speech, even when it comes from a place outside power, because, curled up inside language like a dangerous animal, there lies in ambush a monster, power, the *libido dominandi*, that thousand-headed demon that is language itself.

The nostalgia for silence reappears in an argument of this kind: one can be quiet and stop up one's ears in order not to hear the shoutings of power. And power has a thousand forms, it is not an indivisible totality, as "modern innocence" would like us to believe, for such a division would facilitate the division between those who have power and those who don't. Power and the discourse of power infiltrate all aspects of our lives, even our most private relationships, the most secret areas of individual being, "the liberating impulses which attempt to counteract it."[31] Power, plural and protean, always reemerges, implacable and eternal, in spite of changes and revolutions.

Power, for Barthes, as for Blanchot,[32] is inherent in language, a parasite of the transsocial organism that is language, because language stands on the side of law, it is a form of legislation, and speech is a code. We are forced to live with what is allowed or prohibited by grammar and syntax. Barthes's horror of grammar and syntax is characteristic of an avant-garde attitude, one which, in "Inaugural Lecture," is comparable to positions taken in the review *Tel Quel*. Clearly, Barthes is not only following Mallarmé's questioning of French syntax, and the dictates of surrealism, he is also taking up Queneau's central problem by trying to eliminate the difference between written and spoken language.[33] But Barthes's position is actually less aggressive and more nostalgic: he is gripped by the deep desire for a prelinguistic stage in which language would coincide with the very body, or rather by the desire for an infinite total language, a happy Babel in which all varieties might meet and coexist without any being excluded. His was a nostalgia for a nonformal language, but every language is necessarily formal. Barthes wished a language that conforms to being, and that is a totally concrete consequence, totally dissipated in the innumerable particularities of the concrete. A literary example is Joyce's language, or, to take an example from the Italian tradition, Gadda's, because all dimensions coexist: tradition and the *pastiche* of tradition, oral and obscene language, intimate language and the language of advertising, etc. This nostalgia for a nonformal language seems paradoxical coming from someone who proposed precise methodological requirements for literary criticism, as well as many conceptual abstractions borrowed from linguistics, anthropology, and psychoanalysis. Furthermore, though Barthes's discourse was antisyntactic, his style and writing were actually never subversive in this sense, as he himself noted in *Roland Barthes:* "J'écris classique." His only nonclassical habits in writing consisted in his excessive use of parentheses, dashes, and colons.

Language is harshly assertive and authoritarian. It is only with great difficulty, through the masks of language, that the writer can mold "the implacable power of assertion," intrinsic in syntax and in all stereotypes. Consequently the stereotype is suffocating because it is repetitive, and also because it shows what Barthes calls its gregarious character, that is, the need to be recognized and approved by a group of speakers. In addition, the very structure of language crushes people by forcing them to express themselves according to implacable rules. It is enough to think that direct negation is impossible in many tongues because it requires particular linguistic "operators" that modify the positive sense into the negative one. The paradox faced by the structuralist lies in the fact that structure is oppressive and alienating.

This is perhaps the most threateningly Marxist moment in Barthes: the alienation of language resembles that of the cycle of goods-money-goods which Marx individuated in the economic structure. Strangely enough for one who had complained for years about the stupidity of strong systems and of Marxist stereotypes, Marx reappears as a utopia, a hope, a color, not as a philosophy or a system. Barthes welcomed back the Marxist periodization which identified the second half of the nineteenth century as the crucial moment in the history of European capitalism. His criticism returned to literary history, to the literary histories which are founded on illusory continuities. A "new prophetism" was born, and though it may not have belonged to a free and just society, it was the prophetism of writing. It is politically important, but speaks the truth of being and the truth of utopia. Writing is profoundly realist, because the real is the object of desire, of any desire. But writing is also obstinately unrealistic, exactly because the real is impossible, utopic; so writing desires the impossible and believes that such a desire is sensible:

> This function—perhaps perverse, therefore fitting—has a name: it is the utopian function. Here we come back to History. For it is in the second half of the nineteenth century, one of the grimmest periods of calamitous capitalism, that literature finds its exact figure, at least for us Frenchmen, in Mallarmé. Modernity—our modernity, which begins at this period—can be defined by this new phenomenon: that *utopias of language* are conceived in it. No "history of literature" (if such is still to be written) could be legitimate which would be content, as in the past, to link the various schools together without indicating the gap which here reveals a new prophetic function, that of writing. "To change

language," that Mallarméan expression, is a concomitant of "To change the world," that Marxian one. There is a *political* reception of Mallarmé, of those who have followed him and follow him still.[34]

But Barthes could not abandon himself to this hint of *Tel Quel*, of an avant-garde that believes that language can really change, and change the world. He knew that utopia cannot save one from power, and therefore he reiterated his own words—backward: "The utopia of language is recuperated as the language of utopia—which is a genre like any other."[35]

So the writer who has undertaken the solitary and daily struggle against language will be haunted forever. When he dies, he will be caught by official culture; while he lives he is taken up by fashion, by the images that people continually cast upon him in order to identify him. The writer is caught up in a vortex created by the expectations of those around him.

"I abjure": that was Barthes's response to expectations. "I abjure" signifies a rejection of that which is written, "but not necessarily of that which is thought."[36] Writing cannot rule, because it becomes language again. Perhaps thinking rules, not thinking as ideology or system, but as gray matter, that small part of ourselves we call the brain, the body. Perhaps thinking is the anonymous body of the author, considered in its singularity—and not in its authority, which always originates in the social.

"I abjure": here is the last gesture against language, the extreme wasteland of Barthes's fatigue, of his tending toward the *neuter*, which, in the moment of exaltation, in the pleasure of the text, was a model utopia. For its sake society should have accepted all differences without playing them off against each other, but, in a moment of fatigue, the neuter indicated a return, a fatal turning backward, like Orpheus's. Fatigue represents a recession, a decadent attitude, a regression toward the secret of the body, the style of the writer that Barthes speaks of in

Writing Degree Zero. The neuter is the zero degree, the moment in which one withdraws from everyday struggles, outside of a society hungry for meaning, outside of language that is a social pact. This neutrality of solitude, of a stance outside all power, is literally anarchic; it brings Barthes closer to Camus, the author of Barthes's past, who had a prelinguistic, antisocial idea of the body as dramatically and primordially caught between life and death.

Before language and after language one finds the infant body, and the body that is on the other side of one's own individuality. The latter is not one's own, but one recognizes it all the same; it is the body of lineage, of the *genus.* Such is the body that Barthes finds in looking at family photographs in *Camera Lucida:* a brutal physical mass, the matter which comes to us, from beyond our will, in the line of our ancestors. One also finds death, the body of the dead. Whatever the case, it has to do with the past, the past of the body, of bodies. So how was Barthes to act, if not like Proust who sought to make the past live again in memory, or like Michelet, who sought to make the bodies of the past live again in history?

Thus Barthes, in declaring, in "Inaugural Lecture," the need to abjure, and, in *Camera Lucida*, the noncredibility of the text, came to write of the resurrection that is the phantasm of memory and history, as well as the foundation of photography.

The past returns against language, against that part of language that is held back by writing. It is the past of the body, of photographs of childhood, as in *Roland Barthes*, of the photograph of the mother, as in *Camera Lucida*, and of the writers Barthes loved: Camus, Sartre, Michelet, and Proust.

Science as Phantasm

In *Criticism and Truth*, in which Barthes responded in 1966 to the attacks like those of Raymond Picard and of traditional criticism, Barthes spoke of the science of literature as of something extremely necessary, whose goal "could not be to impose on works a meaning in the name of which one would have the right to reject other meanings . . . ; it would not be a science of contents . . . but a science of the *conditions* of contents, that is, of forms; it would be interested in the variations of meanings that are generated and, I would add, *generatable* by works."[37] The model would be provided by linguistics, especially the transformational linguistics of Chomsky, who set up a hypothetical model of description that could be used as a starting point to explain the ways in which the infinite number of sentences of a language are produced. Not only would a science of literature have to compare literature to myth, which bears no author's signature; it would also have to sacrifice the author, who had been the idol of traditional criticism and the central idea of literary history. In his 1968 article, "The Death of the Author," Barthes greeted the new era of literature by maintaining that "the birth of the reader must be requited by the death of the Author."[38]

I have already said that the death of the author was an ambiguous and provocative idea that seemed to permit the scientific precision of literature and to corrode *auctoritas*, but Barthes, the later Barthes, found himself disowning science and looking for the authors he loved, who were "men and works," or even magical names. Proust's name, for example, is magical for modernity, and for Proust himself the names of certain people and places were magical. Barthes found himself wanting to become an author—and not an authority—that is to say he found himself wanting to write a novel.

The scientific character of literary studies had actually never been totally safe in Barthes's work. In 1967, a year after *Criticism and Truth*, in the article "From Science to Literature," he declared that he was somewhat embarrassed, even pained, because, derived "from a linguistic model, structuralism finds in literature, the work of language, an object much more than affinitary: homogeneous to itself."[39] On the one hand, there is a tendency toward methodology, toward the analytic distance which "a science must keep vis-à-vis its object, without confusing itself with it." On the other hand, there is "the temptation to lose analytic lucidity in the infinity of language." In short, the crucial question remains: structuralism must decide whether it is a science or a writing. And if one of its tasks is to treat literature, then structuralism will be insufficient as long as it remains entirely scientific. In this article, in order to resolve the problem and to avoid saying that structuralism, or at least part of it, was seeking great and beautiful literature—the kind that is light-years away from the positivist realism and the objectivity of the *Nouveau Roman*, a literature, like Proust's, founded on the experience of subjectivity—Barthes proposed the discourse of the theoretical avant-garde: it would then be left to Benveniste's linguistics to make some critical impact by defining the difference between utterance and enunciation. Utterance (*énoncé*) is objective discourse which presents itself as such while negating the idea of an enunciating subject; enunciation (*énonciation*) is discourse in which the subject assumes himself as such in the act of speech. One can thus rediscover all the imposture of a science: it presents itself as founded on absolutely objective discourse, on utterance, and excludes the speaking subject, the act of enunciation. When one reproaches science for its illusions and imaginary objectivity, one necessarily turns it toward writing, because only the latter can openly abolish "the bad faith inherent in every language unaware of its own existence."[40] Once the importance of enunciation has been recognized, then literature will be able to take up an important role among the human sciences, which have always tended to give it a minor position: "The role of literature is to *represent* actively to the scientific institution just what it rejects, i. e., the sovereignty of language."[41]

The scientific enthusiasm of *Criticism and Truth*, and the faith in writing's subversive character vis-à-vis knowledge and science, which Barthes expressed in the 1967 article, were both tied to the conviction that literature should have a progressive role and either become a science or a critique of scientific ideology. Later the terrible idea came that someone who occupies himself with literature must live outside of fashion, in the most absolute *démodé*. This idea was already present in the 1967 article, because Barthes cited Baudelaire speaking of "literary life" as "the sole element in which certain *déclassés* can breathe."[42] In that case, why lie to oneself about the scientific nature of literature or its critical power? One might as well completely accept the *démodé* and take on a *passéiste* attitude, and, alone against the crowd, look for the past, which eludes one like the images of a city where one can no longer find the places and buildings one knew in childhood because the city has since changed.

Thus "Inaugural Lecture," though it borrows Benveniste's terms of utterance and enunciation, has a very different tone from the works of ten or eleven years before. Above all Barthes rejects the contemporary tendency to contest the opposition between sciences and the arts. It sounds good, today, to contest that opposition, Barthes said, immediately indicating his annoyance with the dogma promoting the assimilation of science and literature, a *doxa* that is structuralist in its origin and that Barthes had certainly helped uphold. However, the opposition is not pertinent, especially from the point of view of language, exactly because of the difference between utterance and enunciation: utterance is described in the customary way, as the product of the supposed absence of a speaker, but enunciation is described with an emphasis that makes it colorful and emotional, beyond the abstract subjectivity rightfully belonging to it, beyond the cold style characterizing all objective explanations, even when they speak of the nonobjectivity of the enunciation. Barthes sees in the enunciation what he calls the *energy* of the subject. The term is not used by Benveniste, but comes from Renaissance rhetoric, which designates the force of *inventio*, the act of eloquence in its fullness, that begins even before the *elocutio*, and contains all the persuasiveness of the word's presence: "The act of stating, by exposing the subject's place and energy, even his deficiency (which is not his absence), focuses on the very reality of language, acknowledging that language is an immense halo of implications, of effects, of echoes, of turns, returns, and degrees. It assumes the burden of making understood a subject both insistent and ineffable, unknown and yet recognized by a disturbing familiarity."[43] And Barthes continues in a semiological perspective, remembering that words in the enunciation "are no longer conceived illusively as simple instruments." But this semiological perspective is then broken by the allegory that concludes the paragraph in a crescendo of resumptions: words are "cast as projections, explosions, vibrations, devices, flavors. Writing makes knowledge festive."

Enunciation is writing, the very energy of the subject, a festival of language, which recalls pleasure against the meager convictions of a *doxa*. Even though Barthes stood far from a writer like Rabelais, in the end he was looking for a language as consistent and sensual as the body, for knowledge as joy, as though—on the other side of all absences, of all the voids isolated by structuralism, of all the illusions of the sign found by semiological analysis—he might rediscover the full-bodiedness of the sign capable of attracting all the senses, not only vision, naturally, but also the senses of hearing, smell, touch, and taste.[44] Barthes talks about the taste of words, as one speaks of the taste of food: "In cooking 'things should have the taste of what they are.' "[45] The pagan theme of Dionysian dissoluteness is then seen blinking beneath the sign, or at its heart; it is a theme that has weakened under the influence of modern consciousness. As Genette intuited in "L'Envers des signes," which I have often quoted, the semiologist's secret dream is uncovered, the dream that things should have the taste of what they are (the way, in a good cuisine, the ingredients remain distinct, recognizable). In the realm of knowledge, Barthes said, "it is the taste for words that makes knowledge profound, fecund."[46]

Though all of Barthes's attacks against knowledge are provocative and challenging, they should be taken with a grain of salt. This also applies to his rebellion against the boredom of the Sorbonne and to his deeply humanistic, almost playful and Rabelaisian taste for culture. Literature imposes itself as the orgiastic and pleasurable form of knowledge exactly because it is composed of knowledge. But it does not become dogma, petty pedagogy, sterile or empty erudition; it therefore never takes on the boring, oppressive aspect of knowledge. Criticism—or literary history—becomes intolerable when it aims to found a knowledge of literature and propose literature itself *as* knowledge. What, then, can a writer of criticism do? He can behave not as a critic, but as an essayist, for the essayist stands halfway between the real writer and the academic critic. Or he can break up the form of the essay into fragments or light aphorisms, as Barthes did in *The Pleasure of the Text, Roland Barthes*, and *A Lover's Discourse*.

The essay, an illegitimate genre, was defined in *Roland Barthes* as a form that is condemned to speak with quotation marks, a form that cannot be ironic like the novel. But, in reaction to "literary, lexicological and sociological literature" (the semiology that Barthes was asked to represent at the Collège de France), it is a form that challenged the analytic code of science, it is an "ambiguous genre in which analysis vies with writing," as Barthes said at the beginning of "Inaugural Lecture." By threatening the arrogance of science and truth, the essay as writing offers itself as an affective, emotive space, as value rather than knowledge. This is because in the realm of knowledge one asks "What is it?" about every single thing, whereas value turns that question into "What is it *for me?*"[47] *L'Acoluthia,* Barthes said at the 1977 colloquium "Prétexte: Roland Barthes," is the resolution of contradiction and struggle; it also signifies "the retinue of friends who accompany and guide me, and to whom I entrust myself." Barthes wanted the term to indicate "the rare field where ideas are steeped in affectivity, in which friends, by that retinue which accompanies your life, permit you to think, to write, to speak."[48]

The religion of friendship and the religion of literature: this is the final stage of Barthes's enterprise, because life is so much more delicate and subtle than science. "Literature has an effect of truth much more violent for me than that of religion. By which I mean, quite simply, that literature is *like* religion."[49]

Barthesian semiology is and was a process of apprenticeship. As such it went through two periods: one of illusion and one of disillusion. At the moment of disillusion, the old illusion appears to be a mistake, a blunder. But disillusion does not lead to total bitterness. On the contrary, it becomes a productive force that pushes one to look for other solutions, to reevaluate the past more deeply, to rediscover meanings beyond the farce of meaning, the semantic incrustations. For example, having attacked biographical criticism, one can reinvent biography, as in *Roland Barthes*, or having rejected sentimentalism, one can turn and face sentiment squarely, as in *Camera Lucida*.

The project of semiology as science, inspired by Saussurian linguistics, was founded on the distinction between language and discourse (*langue* and *parole*), not only because distinctions are necessary to science, but also because within the limits of this position it seems possible to dominate the entire generality of language, to capture the structure which makes all events susceptible to rationalization. In his inaugural lecture at the Collège de France, Barthes remarked on the way in which he would use almost interchangeably the terms *discours* and *langue:* discourse and language now seem indivisible to him. The distinction had once previously served the purposes of his research, but now it is something to be abjured. Linguistics and semiology are suddenly seen to be going in totally different directions, with the first following a scientific or mathematical path, and the second an emotional one. Like literature, like the nineteenth-century novel, semiology deals with the human passions. Barthes declares in fact that linguistics now seems to him to "be working on an enormous imposture, on an object [discourse] it makes improperly clean and pure."[50] Semiology would then be the work of the impure, of that which corrupts the supposed purity of the message, "nothing less than the desires, the fears, the appearances, the intimidations, the advances, the blandishments, the protests, the excuses, the aggressions, the various kinds of music out of which active language is made."[51]

Barthes is aware of how personal and individual his definition is, of how it moves in a direction opposite to the one taken by semiology today—the positive science of the sign—in reviews, universities, and associations. Barthes wants, instead, to go toward the passions, toward *feeling*.

Paradoxically, semiology rediscovered the distinction made by Gustave Lanson, the father of French literary history: "One should distinguish 'knowledge' from 'feeling,' that which can be known from that which must be felt; one should not feel there where one can know, and should not believe he knows when he feels: I believe that the scientific method of literary history can be reduced to this."[52] Anti-Lansonian, Barthes chose to go toward feeling, knowing that this choice had been filtered through the myth of science, that of Saussure's and Benveniste's linguistics: the latter excited his enthusiasm because it allowed him to found "scientifically," within language itself, the idea that the subject does not exist, but is only an instance of discourse. But active language and real life restore the subject not as a full, rational form, not as *cogito*, but as wounded sensitivity, as emotional subjectivity which gives words a range of passions going from tenderness to aggression.

When there is an attempt to fuse knowledge and feeling, one is likely to prevail over the other. Consequently,

Barthes's early semiology, even though it went against traditional knowledge, was stronger on the side of knowledge, whereas his later semiology, which overlapped with literature while it played and fused all forms of knowledge, necessarily hinted at feeling. It was against intelligence.

Proust

It is our passions which outline our books, and the periods of rest in between which write them.—Marcel Proust

It would, however, be an error to take this opposition to intelligence literally. Even here Barthes had a vaguely rebellious attitude. His rebellion was never polemical, never directed against anyone in particular, as he detested struggle, the *maché* of languages; he always rebelled against dogma, *doxa*—in this case the *doxa* of scientific semiology. Barthesian rebellion was always and only directed against language. On the other hand, when he was at the Collège de France, Barthes upheld the value of intelligence, saying, in a passage already cited, that "intellectual conversions are the very pulsion of intelligence." The term "pulsion" serves to remind us that intelligence is a subjective fact that has been affected by emotivity.

To rationalize what is emotional and to make emotional that which is intellectual: the gulf that lies between the two is a gulf between intelligence and sensibility, between heart and brain, a chasm which Hofmannsthal had already proposed (as had Freud and Klimt in Vienna at the beginning of the century). Lord Chandos maintained that "we could enter in a new and hopeful relationship with the whole of existence if only we begin to think with the heart."[53] And if we begin to feel with the brain, so we must continue Chandos's sentence. This gulf between feeling and intelligence is the figure that enables one to overcome the positivist oppositions of Taine and Lanson. Barthes had looked for such a gulf. He tried in all possible ways to find the language, the words, the sentences which could describe it, words which, as Lord Chandos would say, "would make the cherubim, in whom I do not believe, fall stone dead." *Camera Lucida* realizes this ideal (at least in all of the second part). Here the terms *"studium"* and *"punctum"* are used to describe the effects of photography. The former indicates that which belongs to the order of rationality, knowledge, and culture, in short, to the order of intelligence, whereas the second refers to that which belongs to the emotional order. This distinction, which is useful and didactic, does not, however, overcome the structuralist habit of proceeding in binary terms. Moreover, it was the price that Barthes had to pay in order to remain faithful to his work's subtitle (*Note sur la photographie*), as though the book were about photography, when the truth is that this last book of Barthes is about his mother. It was his own small version of *A la recherche du temps perdu*. The real argument of the book, the real new language can be found in its second part, where every page is *thought* with emotion—with the heart, as Lord Chandos would say.

It would be a mistake to negate the role of the intelligence in the later Barthes, just as it would be a mistake to take literally Proust's objections to intelligence when, in *Contre Sainte-Beuve*, he speaks of the purely casual relationships which are brought about by memory: "Every day I consider intelligence less important. Every day I realize that only outside intelligence the writer can hold to something of our past impressions, which is to say that he can reach something of himself and the true matter of art. What intelligence gives us under the name of past is not our past."[54] Certainly, even in *Le Temps retrouvé*, at the very moment when the narrator is discovering his artistic vocation, Proust is suspicious of intelligence, though the truths that it gathers are very valuable: "They are like drawings with a hard outline and no perspective," they are flat, without thickness or depth, by virtue of the fact that "they have not been re-created." But the narrator adds: "I felt, however, that these truths which the intellect educes directly from reality were not altogether to be despised." In fact they contain a matter that is "imbued with mind," which can accompany the work of art, and they help to compose it together with the most precious sensations, which "are also too rare for a work of art to be constructed exclusively from them."[55] In short, the work of art is a tissue of material given by intelligence and by deep feeling, then recreated in the subject.

It would be a mistake to believe that Proust did not value intelligence. Such a reading of the *Recherche* would give too much importance to the brief experiences of involuntary memory. It would also ignore the value of *Le Temps retrouvé*, which asks one to reread the entire novel as a learning of signs, possible only in time as duration. But the *Recherche*, as Paul Ricoeur wrote,[56] is a "fable of time," and Proust himself said as much in an interview he gave in the 13 November 1913 issue of *Le Temps*, at the time of the publication of *Du côté de chez Swann*. The novel "is not only a plane psychology but a temporal psychology [in the same way that one speaks of a plane geometry and a spatial geometry]. I have tried to isolate such a substance, invisible in time, but for this it was necessary that experience might last."[57]

My digression on Proust has the precise aim of showing what has already been suggested, that the later Barthes, in spite of the structuralist ideology of the death of the author, rediscovered the authors he loved, and among them Proust held a privileged position. Proust represented for him, in all his work, a desire and a mistake, the very mistake that led him to identify writing, as conceived by structuralism, with fiction and the novel. Paradoxically, and contrary to his own statements, Barthes was not a writer of novels, but a critic, and since the two terms are confused for all the reasons and needs of the modern, as I have illustrated, one will see that Barthes took the side of art and literature, not so much as an artist, but rather as a critic or moralist. One could also say that he was the perfect figure of the essayist and that he reached the ideal stage of the form of the essay (*Camera Lucida*) at the very moment when he expressed his desire to write a novel. Barthes completed a course that was the opposite of that of Proust, who, when he thought he was writing an essay against the methods of Taine and Sainte-Beuve, was actually beginning his novel. When Barthes expressed his desire to write a novel, he wrote a lyrical essay—the lyric is founded on the "I," on the attempt to give a voice to things and beings.

In Barthes's theoretical texts the name of Proust often appears alongside those of Mallarmé and Flaubert. It is used to indicate a turning point in modern literature, when the history of the decision to write became the very story of the novel. The literary work thus tells the condition of its birth. But when Barthes spoke of Proust, he did not sound very much like a critic speaking about an author: the only texts in this direction are "Proust and the Names," written in 1967 (now in *New Critical Essays*), and "An Idea of Research," written in 1971 (now in *The Rustle of Language*). In the latter article Barthes reads the *Recherche* as "a form of discourse whose very obsessiveness is enigmatic,"[58] something like inversion, the reversal of situations, opinions, values, emotions—for example, Swann, who is the friend of princes, is not a high-class individual for the narrator's aunts. In his 1967 article Barthes took Proustian onomatology as the point of departure for the *Recherche*, confirming Lévi-Strauss's thesis on the meaning of the proper name.

These essays belong to the very canonical French tradition of criticism, and can be situated in the wake of Sainte-Beuve's *Nouveaux Lundis* or Taine's *Essais de critique et d'histoire* (these works initiated the tradition of journalistic literary criticism, before the monumental work of Lanson appeared on the scene). This kind of brief essay does not pretend to treat an author exhaustively, but tries to place an author or a text in relation to the great systems of an era. Just as Taine and Sainte-Beuve borrowed organic metaphors from natural sciences, critics of the 1960s used scientific terminology and concepts from structuralist linguistics and anthropology, two sciences essential to the twentieth century, as anatomy and biology had been to the nineteenth century.

Even more important than these brief studies of Proust was the lecture "Longtemps, je me suis couché de bonne heure," given in 1978, and the following statement about Proust, made in *The Pleasure of the Text:*

> I recognize that Proust's work, for myself at least, is *the* reference work, the general *mathesis,* the *mandala* of the entire literary cosmogony—as Madame de Sévigné's letters were for the narrator's grandmother, tales of chivalry for Don Quixote, etc.; this does not mean that I am in any way a Proust "specialist": Proust is what comes to me, not what I summon up; not an "authority," simply a *circular memory.* Which is what the inter-text is: the impossibility of living outside the infinite text—whether this text be Proust or the daily newspaper or the television screen: the book creates the meaning, the meaning creates life.[59]

This passage holds *in nuce* Barthes's relationship to Proust in his later years. It illustrates the character of a relationship that was neither scholarly nor intellectual, but dwelled in emotions ranging from the pleasure of reading to the pain experienced on his mother's death—in an experience of time both as moment and duration.

One ought to keep in mind the form of inversion that Barthes discussed in "An Idea of Research." The great reversal of Barthes's attraction for Proust is exactly that of pleasure into pain, that of reading into writing (from reading into writing: wasn't this the trajectory followed by the narrator of the *Recherche?*). This reversal is the final conversion of Barthes, who, in "Longtemps, je me suis couché de bonne heure," spoke insistently of a *Vita Nuova.* For

Barthes, who had defined himself as an author of essays in "Inaugural Lecture," this *Vita Nuova* was represented by his intention to write a novel, by the announcement of a novel the authority of which would reside in "the truth of affects, not of ideas: hence, [the novel] is never arrogant, terrorist: according to Nietzsche's typology, it aligns itself with Art, not with Priesthood."[60]

The surprise, the *ethos* of Proustian inversion, Barthes says in "An Idea of Research," "is the astonishment of a *return*, a *junction*, a *recognition*."[61] It is, in short, the surprise of a concomitant syntax that unites opposites. For example, the Princess Sherbatoff, who seemed extremely vulgar to the traveling narrator, is *only* the madam of a brothel; but, according to a concomitant or circular syntax, she is both the madam of a brothel and a princess. The circular syntax leads Barthes to the recognition of his "vocation": he wanted to write a novel. He had always wanted to be a writer. This wish was present in *Writing Degree Zero*, explicit in the sentence printed on the cover of *Roland Barthes*—"All this should be considered as though it had been written by a fictional character"—and implicit in Barthes's interest in enunciation, true as desire, but neither as form nor as practice.

The narrator of the *Recherche*, though he is afraid he will not have the time to write, will in fact write, in a future that becomes real because the narrator has as his double the writer who has actually written the novel. Barthes, on the other hand, was a professor condemned to the spoken word and most often to a writing that originated in speaking and teaching; he expressed his desire to write a novel, but did not have the time, and left only critical essays. This is a cruel joke played by time. On the other hand, Barthes was aware of the joke, because he defined his novel as a phantasm, as probably impossible and utopian.

Return and rediscovery are figures of time, they take shape in time, in the circularity of Barthes's works, at the moment in which he is getting older and time is pressing, as for Proust when he was ill:

There comes a time (and this is a problem of consciousness) when "our days are numbered"; there begins a backwards count, vague yet irreversible. You *knew* you were mortal (everyone has told you so, ever since you had ears to hear); suddenly you *feel* mortal (this is not a natural feeling: the natural one is to believe yourself immortal: whence so many accidents due to carelessness). This evidence, once it is experienced, transforms the landscape: I must, imperatively, lodge my work in a compartment which has uncertain contours but which I know (new consciousness) are *finite:* the last compartment.[62]

This whole paragraph echoes Proust:

And now I began to understand what old age was—old age, which perhaps of all the realities is the one of which we preserve for longest in our life a purely abstract conception, looking at calendars, dating our letters, seeing our friends marry and then in their turn the children of our friends, and yet, either from fear or from sloth, not understanding what all this means, until the day when we behold an unknown silhouette, like that of M. d'Argencourt, which teaches us that we are living in a new world; . . . and I began to understand too what death meant and love and the joys of the spiritual life, the usefulness of suffering, a vocation, etc.[63]

In his preface to *The Life of Rancé* written in 1965, Barthes used a sentence of Chateaubriand's as an epigraph: "Je ne suis plus que le temps." "I am no longer anything but time." The subject of *The Life of Rancé* is old age, and Barthes remarked that such a subject disappeared from modern works, where mostly the child or the adolescent has a literary status. But, in a sort of fascination for the *déclassés* which recalls Baudelaire's fascination for old women or men (in poems like "Les Petites Vieilles" and "Les Sept Vieillards"), Barthes remarked that old age can "move us quite as much as a love story."[64] By a strange coincidence, the experience of time is affected by a return to the self, the work is felt as lodging the most mysterious, deep self, that "little thing that is himself," as Barthes said in *Roland Barthes*. The experience of time is also affected by the very figure of inversion (according to which the Princess Sherbatoff is *also* a vulgar woman). Time as duration is perceived as opposite and parallel to the impossibility of duration characteristic of Barthes's early work, *Writing Degree Zero*, where literary forms are immediately engulfed by history: opposite because duration opposes itself to the instant, the way the *imparfait* opposes itself to the *passé simple*, and parallel because, as Barthes said in "An Idea of Research," "to *utter* the contraries is finally to *unite* them in the very unity of the text, in the writing's journey."[65]

The hero of the *Recherche* again sees, in a dramatic reversal, the places and episodes of the past in another light, exactly because they now carry the stamp of art. Similarly, Barthes, in a dramatic reversal provoked by the concurrence of his weariness of intellectual fashions and the death of his mother, rediscovers writing to be not only a struggle against stereotype, but a movement against death itself, an attempt to tear from death "those I love," to *speak them*, in order to rescue them from oblivion. Barthes passes from language to being, from language as a formal reality or unreality to the tormented, delirious relationship between language and the world, from the problem of style as technique to the problem of style as vision.

Such a situation is Proustian indeed: it is the situation in which the writer conceives of the indissoluble link between literature and life, and attributes to art the power to know life as reality, to recreate it on the other side of the superficial and conventional knowledge we have of it: "Real life, life at last laid bare and illuminated—the only life in consequence which can be said to be really lived—is literature . . . But art, if it means awareness of our own life, means also awareness of the lives of other people—for style for the writer, no less than colour for the painter, is a question not of technique but of vision."[66]

For Proust the work of the artist—his "struggle to discern beneath matter"—implies a *reversal* of the banality and blindness of everyday life: it is "a process exactly the reverse of that which, in those everyday lives which we live with our gaze averted from ourselves, is at every moment being accomplished by vanity and passion and the intellect, and habit too."[67]

Proust's circular memory, which Barthes speaks of in *The Pleasure of the Text*, continues to grow stronger, and one could read many of the later Barthes's statements as echoes of certain of Proust's sentences, especially from *Le Temps retrouvé*, not because Barthes was a specialist in Proust, but because Barthes identified with Proust in the exact same way that the narrator identifies with his own memories: "Does this mean I am offering you a lecture 'on' Proust? Yes and no. My subject will be, if you like, *Proust and I*. How pretentious! . . . Let me suggest that, paradoxically, the pretentiousness subsides once I myself take the stand, and not some witness: by setting Proust and myself on one and the same line, I am not in the least comparing myself to this great writer, but, quite differently, *identifying myself with him:* an association of practice, not of value."[68]

For Barthes, Proust must have been what Vergil was for Dante: an *exemplum*. Barthes proposed the most typical and classical adventure of the reading of fiction, that of identification. Thus he presented himself as an ordinary reader, and not as a Proust specialist. Furthermore, he let us understand that his identification with Proust was linked to a game involving a triple system of masks: in Proust, identification with the author and identification with the work blend in a distinctive way because Proust is doubled in Marcel who wants to write and in Marcel who does write, and because all of the *Recherche* is the narrative of a desire to write. But, above all, since *Le Temps retrouvé* hinges on the revelation of the hero who, according to the logic of reversal, discovers his vocation as a writer at the moment when he no longer believes in it, Barthes wishes to convey that his *Vita Nuova* is to be understood as a true conversion.

The novel not only represents the last stage of his eclecticism, which had brought him to subscribe to different systems simultaneously, to dream often "of a peaceful coexistence of critical languages,"[69] and to try different forms of writing, including the fragment. The novel constitutes a true revelation of literature as a representation of reality, as lived life. As such it puts a little distance between loved ones and death, and it also keeps us from eternally repeating the same actions: writing articles, running errands, giving lectures, forever, until death. Sisyphus was not happy; repetition is the very figure of fatigue: again and again, every day, but when will it end? The novel becomes a job for the critic, and for the professor it becomes the form that manages to escape, at least a little, from Sisyphus's hell; or it could be the labor of Sisyphus seen by the mass which undertakes Sisyphus's journey in reverse and undoes the work which, as Proust says, "is at every moment accomplished by vanity and passion and the intellect," by "our spirit of imitation, our abstract intelligence, our habits."[70] On the contrary, Proust continues, it is work for which one needs "courage of many kinds, including the courage of one's own emotions." Barthes had this kind of sentimental courage in mind when he went looking for the novel that speaks of passions in a world where one must hide tenderness, a modern intellectual world in which all morality scorns and condemns *pathos*. For this, one needs the courage to be *démodé*.

At a certain point, the novel, which is the ideal form of Barthesian work that I spoke of in the first chapter, and which resembles Michelet's work, the novel or the idea of the novel, while participating in conversion, while being understood as a new beginning, retraces the old pathways and leads one to read all of Barthes from a novelistic perspective, as leading to a desire to write fiction. We know how the term "fiction" has accompanied the adventure of the term "writing," the triumph of the signifier, and without referring to Philippe Sollers or Julia Kristeva, we can remember how insistently Lacan spoke of the pleasure of fiction regarding the stage of the mirror. In *Roland Barthes*, Barthes dedicates a few of his fragments to fiction. First he defines it as a kind of mania for tracing, thereby linking it to the image of style as vision, in order to ask himself whether science cannot have visions and become *fictional*: "Fiction would proceed from a *new intellectual art* (which is how semiology and structuralism are defined in *Système de la mode*). With intellectual things we produce simultaneously theory, critical combat, and pleasure."[71] Barthes asks himself questions in order to conclude this fragment of *Roland Barthes* with the statement that he himself "would have wanted to produce not a comedy of the Intellect, but its *romanesque*, its novelistic theory."

Barthes, here, was dreaming of fiction—which comes close to what he defined as romanesque in order to escape the term "novel" ("*roman*"), consecrated by literary history—before the prophecy of his *Vita Nuova*. But the time came when he was no longer afraid to take up the old terms and to say, openly, "novel," using the standard term, in order to signal that it was time to question modern manias. This great reversal was not terminological, and cannot be minimized by a substitution of jargonistic keywords. Barthes no longer wanted to write "the romanesque of the intellect," but a novel that would represent passion and *pathos*.

Paradoxically, at the end of the twentieth century, the semiologist, following the intuition of his *Vita Nuova*, conscious of an event that has changed his life, finds himself in a certain sense in a condition which is the opposite of Lord Chandos's—and nevertheless this does not destroy the association with him that I have maintained throughout this study; it simply reverses it, according to the rule of writing which unites the opposites, or to the rule of Proust's circular syntax. In fact, Bacon's friend signaled the emergence of the modern and tried to make the most marginal, voiceless things—like rats, or a bug—speak the language of silence, whereas Barthes signaled the return of the *démodé* and sought to shelter beings with a voice from the silence of death. He tried to give them back their voice, the way that Michelet tried to give a voice back to the dead of history.

In any case, there is perhaps in all that is written a circular syntax leading us to say that there is a deep complicity, which began with Baudelaire, between the modern and the *démodé*: this crucial point of coincidence makes the very quality of that which is decadent, without becoming decadence itself, exactly because it has to do, not with a school, but with an individual experience. Such is the destiny of that which begins with an avant-garde or challenging impulse, like Proust who began by writing against Sainte-Beuve: to rediscover the classical and the *démodé*, to feel the cruel nostalgia of things ending, of time passing.

Once again Barthes found himself in a Proustian situation, like the narrator who, at the moment when he has become indifferent to death, finds that it represents a grave danger for his book, and states the law of art: "To me it seems more correct to say that the cruel law of art is that people die and we ourselves die after exhausting every form of suffering, so that over our heads may grow the grass not of oblivion, but of eternal life, the vigorous and luxuriant growth of a true work of art, and so that thither, gaily and without a thought for those who are sleeping beneath them, future generations may come to enjoy their *déjeuner sur l'herbe*."[72] The law of art is the law of time and suffering.

Suffering

But, like Elstir Chardin, one cannot redo what one loves without giving it up.—Marcel Proust

Barthes's lecture on Proust and the novel, that form both Proust and Barthes were seeking, ends with a question: won't the novel have to "express at once the world's brilliance and the world's suffering, all that beguiles and offends me?"[73] This rhetorical question echoes, in changed form, the already cited final sentence of Barthes's article on Foucault's *Madness and Civilization*, where, according to Barthes, writing comes with a glimmer of dangerous power, a tragedy, in a kind of amazement over newness, ancient newness: "A vertigo which appears not only upon contact with madness, but indeed each time that man, taking his distances, observes the world as different, which is to say each time he writes."[74] But in the older essay the final spark rose out of the bad faith which, for Barthes, is necessary to any form of knowledge, and inherent to discourse on discourse. Any metalanguage implies an ambiguous position, which is a way of looking at the world "not as an object but as a writing," and Barthes maintains his wish to abolish discourse on discourse. However, the novel, that new and uncertain form, is, through the Proustian device of inversion, devoid of all bad faith, because it does not pressure the reader, inasmuch as it seeks to represent the truth of emotions and not of ideas.

Barthes wondered whether he would really write the novel of emotions that he wished to, and he wondered if he really ought to call it a novel. Paradoxically he was more certain of its contents (passion) and its aim (to rescue loved ones from oblivion) than of its form. Such a novel, or essay on the novel, would avoid bad faith because its content would be without bad faith. It would stand beyond the egoism of the intellect that mirrors itself and its own journeys, an egoism inherent to discourse on discourse. Discourse on discourse is a narcissistic exercise. Narcissism is a completely intellectual, reflexive operation, like looking at one's own image, while affection necessarily goes toward the *other*, toward the other as real absence, because the novel tries to speak of loved ones who are now dead. The novel must become the tangible form or container of suffering.

As for its form, one can ask: will it be fragmentary, aphoristic, or will it uphold the narrative continuity characterizing the traditional novel? Will it be able to join these two tendencies?

The Proustian figure of inversion comes back again, this time in Barthes's life, and a certain reversal results, depicting a conversion no longer as a point of rupture, a crucial moment *nel mezzo del cammin,* but as a tension that had always been there, explicit or hidden: that of writing, the obsessive term in Barthes's work. Once again, a reading that analyzes Barthes according to a logic of development or change, of periodization, merges with a reading that rediscovers the insistence of an obsessive theme—like Barthes's interpretation of Michelet.

The syntax of reversal came into the picture later on. Barthes became aware that he was speaking of the novel *as if* he had to write one, at the time when he left science far behind, at a moment in which, thanks to the *démodé,* a new humanism (to use his expression that dates back to 1962) was suggested and the truth of the emotions was being proclaimed. *As if,* according to the formula used by scientific enterprise and implying "something to do" instead of speaking of what others had done: "Perhaps it is finally at the heart of this subjectivity, of this very intimacy which I have invoked, perhaps it is at the 'pinnacle of my particularity' that I am scientific without knowing it, vaguely oriented toward that *Scienza Nuova* Vico spoke of."[75] The repetition of *as if* highlights both subjectivity and science as forms of the affections, as expressions "of the world's brilliance and the world's suffering."

Barthes wrote a book in which he tried to sketch out a possible science of the subject that would avoid prevaricating individuality as well as reductive generalities that crush the particular: *Camera Lucida* is such a book, such a *new science.*

After reading "Longtemps, je me suis couché de bonne heure," one should not expect the novel that Barthes would have liked to write but never did, one should not hope that unedited manuscripts will turn up to fulfill our expectations. *Incidents* with its fragments, its tone of a *journal intime*, is not realizing Barthes's utopia of fictional writing; it is not the book of his *as if*. That strange form, which, as Barthes said at the end of his lecture, "Longtemps, je me suis couché de bonne heure," had to break "with the uniformly intellectual nature of my previous writings (even if a number of fictive elements taint their rigor),"[76] was actually produced by Barthes. The work does exist, as a product of suffering, as a *new science* that penetrates into the deepest areas of subjectivity and intimacy, into the particularity of the subject, dense and limpid like "the ineffable which is resolved in a formal key," of which Proust spoke apropos of style in *Contre Sainte-Beuve*.[77] It is the last book Barthes wrote before his death, *Camera Lucida*, a text born of his mother's death and nourished by it.

Camera Lucida is a miraculously synthetic text: brief, transparent, and clear. One could say about it what Barthes himself said about Benveniste: "There is a beauty, an experience of the intellect, which gives the work of certain scholars that *inexhaustible clarity* which also goes into the making of great literary works."[78]

Camera Lucida is not a novel, but a new form that breaks, on the level of argumentation, with the uniformly intellectual character of Barthes's previous writings: the argument is in fact emotional and shows the emotional, personal foundation of any intellectual enterprise. On the level of technique, *Camera Lucida*'s style is fragmentary, but respects the continuity of chronology or rather temporality. The first part of the book, in fact, opens with "*Un jour il y a bien longtemps*" ("One day, quite some time ago"), an adverbial phrase which engulfs the narrative in the precise point at which a scene founds memory, drawing upon all the nuances of the *passé simple*. The *passé simple* had already been studied in *Writing Degree Zero* as the typical tense of the novel ("Writing and the Novel"). The narrative in *Camera Lucida* is the story of an intellectual process, it describes for us the first time that Roland Barthes, a long time ago, began to ask himself questions about photography—on seeing a picture of Napoleon's brother. The second part of *Camera Lucida* opens with another temporal sentence—"One November evening shortly after my mother's death"—which introduces the unexpected rediscovery of a picture representing his mother as a child in a winter garden. This picture gave him the truth and very being of his mother along with a consciousness of her death.

Camera Lucida is, therefore, a miraculously synthetic text, a brief literary work gathering together all the intellectual and affective themes and tensions found in Barthes's work.

The great linguistic-structuralist wave that characterized the intellectual, the mythologist, and the semiologist is already present in the object being analyzed, photography. Photography is in fact an art or technique congenial to a structuralist approach because of its communicative importance in the contemporary world and because it can be analyzed in terms founded on a binary opposition of a linguistic kind—that of *studium* and *punctum*, which is not too unlike that of denotation and connotation. Photography has already been studied in early essays, "The Photographic Message" (1961) and "The Rhetoric of Image" (1964), now in *The Responsibility of Forms* (the first part of *Camera Lucida* develops the argument of the 1964 essay). Furthermore, photography, like love in *A Lover's Discourse*, is a privileged focus from which one can continue to investigate the imaginary and its ties to the idea of subjectivity—the photo would be the image par excellence, the way my reflection in a mirror is an image. Studying photography can also help to elaborate some of Benveniste's ideas so important for Barthes, like the difference between the subject of utterance (*énoncé*) and the subject of enuncia-tion (*énonciation*). Barthes, having tried various pro-nominal masks, from "I" to "he" in *Roland Barthes*, writes now a book in the first-person singular, thereby completely assuming the act of speech, the subject of *énonciation*.

But the figure of reversal in the syntax of concomitance is always at work: then there is a return to the most remote segment of Barthes's intellectual past, that is, Sartre's phe-nomenology, and to the author whom we have already seen as representing his *mathesis* and his point of identification, Proust. There is also the dedication to Sartre—the dedica-tion being, in Barthes's words, "a figure of the lover's dis-course."[79] There are the innumerable Proustian reminis-cences: the sign of the return, a transversal and almost affective return, linked to an act of homage and the sense of a debt. Barthes does not write a study on Sartre, just as he does not write on Proust, but he passes through the beautiful sentences of one and the philosophical intentions of the other. Such movement is not only one of grounding but also one of remembering, rediscovering the fundamen-tal impressions that compose the self. Such movement im-plies a deep consciousness of oneself, of the other, and of time, all fusing in the same way the most diverse colors can melt into each other in barely perceptible shades.

Chateaubriand is never mentioned in *Camera Lucida*, but he is briefly recalled in "Longtemps, je me suis couché de bonne heure," since Rancé is an example of that trans-formation of landscape or mutation of existence Barthes talks about: "Rancé, hero of the Fronde, a worldly dandy, comes from his travels and discovers the body of his mis-tress, decapitated by an accident: he withdraws from the world . . . For Proust, the 'middlelife's journey' was cer-tainly his mother's death."[80] Unexpectedly, secretly, with *Camera Lucida*, Barthes finds himself in the prophetic posi-tion he described, in 1965, as being the one of Chateaubri-and: "His *Life of Rancé* is prophetically experienced as his last work, and twice over, he identifies himself with Poussin dying in Rome (the city of ruins) and depositing in his last painting that mysterious and sovereign imperfection, lovelier than a merely fulfilled art and which is the *tremor of time*: memory is the beginning of writing, and writing is in its turn the beginning of death (however young one is when he undertakes it)."[81]

Not unlike Chateaubriand, who identified with Poussin, Barthes identified with Proust, as he said in "Longtemps, je me suis couché de bonne heure," and, maybe, simply because his mother's death provoked a mutation of existence. Like Chateaubriand, whose *Mémoires d'outre-tombe* he re-read in 1979,[82] the year before his death, Barthes deposits in his last work the *tremor* of time: himself when he started thinking about photography, his mother, the past of his mother, the writers he loved and loves.

Proust and Sartre, in spite of all that makes them incompatible, coexist in Barthes's research as though in a circular syntax, if only through the idea of research leading to Proust's novel and Sartre's philosophy. And then they coexist thanks to a comprehensive conception of subjectivity, linked to conscience and will, the existentialist will to exist and the Proustian will to write: simple and general ideas that have nothing to do, for example, with the minute and sophisticated work of deconstructionist critics, like Jacques Derrida and Paul de Man, who always pay more attention to the problematic knots in a thought, or to the subtle and contradictory ideas glimmering in half a sentence or in a tangled remark springing from Kant or Heidegger. Barthes, on the other hand, behaves like an artist when he is dealing with elements that are intellectually general or reduced to essential facts. He enriches them with images rather than ideas, in the same way that a painter works with the few basic colors of a palette and magically transforms them on his canvas, creating colors of a refined or violent quality.

Barthes behaves like the writer that Proust speaks of in *Le*

Temps retrouvé, the one who, without knowing it, without resorting to the punctilious sophistications of the intelligence, has managed to capture in gestures, movements, accents, and spaces something which renews itself and lasts:

> There is a feeling for generality which, in the future writer, itself picks out what is general and can for that reason one day enter into a work of art. And this has made him listen to people only when, stupid or absurd though they may have been, they have turned themselves, by repeating like parrots what other people of similar character are in the habit of saying, into birds of augury, mouthpieces of a psychological law. He remembers only things that are general. By such tones of voice, such variations in the physiognomy, seen perhaps in the early childhood, has the life of other people been represented for him and when, later, he becomes a writer, it is from these observations that he composes his human figures, grafting on to a movement of shoulders common to a number of people—a movement as truthfully delineated as though it had been recorded in an anatomist's note-book, though the truth which he uses it to express is of a psychological order—a movement of the neck made by someone else, each of many individuals having posed for a moment as his model.[83]

From Proust to Sartre, Barthes took the most general things that can be said and repeated by people who speak "like parrots," but in a way that was nonetheless prophetic, that nonetheless formulated a law. He superimposed a movement made by one onto a movement made by the other and onto other movements as well, thus composing various poses with diverse models. In this way Barthes, to continue Proust's metaphor, places the movement of Lacan's psychoanalysis on the "shoulders" of Sartre's phenomenology. Sartre spoke of the imaginary as the absence of the real, Lacan of the real as that which is impossible, unseizable, and lacking. Barthes added these generalities of an intellectual order not only to the great generality of Proust—memory—but also to several essential scenes in the *Recherche*, which are explicitly or implicitly quoted in *Camera Lucida*. One finds again, for example, the sense of anguishing truth, of strange contradiction in which, in *Sodome et Gomorrhe*, the feeling of nothingness is mixed with the feeling of survival when the hero, bending over to undo his boots, is suddenly struck by a vivid and acute memory of his dead grandmother: her piercing presence is recreated by memory and completely made of absence. The parallel for Barthes lies in his painful perception of his own mother's death, and photography, one photograph in particular, that of his mother as a child, the photo of the winter garden, is the *medium* of that revelation. It becomes the equivalent of all that constitutes the essence of photographic art. Only the emotivity of the subject, who finds himself in a singular and concrete object, legitimates the truth of a science, some knowledge of Photography: here one finds realized the old dream of science as fiction, of science capable of visions, which had been expressed in the previously cited fragment on fiction in *Roland Barthes*.

Just as, for Proust, an artist must have seen many bell towers in order to describe a particular bell tower, so must Barthes's research be composed of innumerable elements, musical notes that chase after one another, combine and echo one another. Then authors and scattered quotations become enchanting names or images, as memories are images, and so are photographs. In this way Nietzsche, who was so important for Barthes's style and thinking—or the images of his thinking—becomes a myth in *Camera Lucida*, the way Orpheus and Sisyphus are myths. Nietzsche, the extreme and desperately modern figure of *pietas* who stood at the edge of insanity, is depicted as someone throwing himself on the neck of a martyred horse—crazy with piety. This piety figures the very impulse of Barthes, who was induced to see photography not only as an image, the light shadow of the loved body, but as the very reality of that little bit of body it represents. The insanity of piety also constituted the scandalous vision that Benjamin so much liked in *The Letter of Lord Chandos:* Crasso in tears over the death of his lamprey.

Had Barthes really found the *noema* of photography in *Camera Lucida?* Yes and no, the way, in his lecture at the Collège de France, he had tried to speak of himself and of Proust. If one looks at the work as a type of essay, then yes, Barthes was speaking of photography indeed, and of its resistance to semiotics as the positive science of the sign; but if one sees it as a form related to the novel, then he was speaking of his mother.

In *A Lover's Discourse*, Barthes said he had tried to treat love in a way that would be different from psychoanalysis, and he particularized it in figures, instead of making it abstract. In *Camera Lucida* Barthes spoke of his mother, and went beyond the psychoanalytic definitions of the mother-son relationship. The *imago*, the imaginary that for Lacan defines such a relationship, is gradually excluded in favor of the real, the unavoidable *res:* death.

But symbolism, the abstract law that dominates Lacan's thought, is also softened, because Barthes was looking for *his* mother, not the Mother. The power of representation returns against abstract theory and formulas. Barthes recalled that Judaism rejected the image in order to avoid the risk of adoring the Mother, whereas Christianity, thanks to the representation of the Mother, overcame "the rigor of the Law for the sake of the Image-Repertoire [*l'Imaginaire*]."[84] Barthes, coming from a religious culture (Protestantism) that has no cult of the mother, "but doubtless formed culturally by Catholic art," let himself go to the fullness of the Image and the Imaginary; for that very reason he understood it and sought to escape. There only remains the real, the third term of Lacan's triad (the symbolic, the imaginary, and the real). As it was for Proust, the only truth is art, which tries to represent the real, which can only capture it in the fleeting moment. Thus Baudelaire saw the passerby and gave himself over to the cult of images, to art's power of representation. The novel that Barthes desired is "representation and not expression,"[85] that is, an attempt to grasp the presence that is always escaping into time, and not only into space, as the passerby into Baudelaire's city. The novel is the form representing time, its ineluctable corrosive power affecting any presence, any reality. Time in space, in the space of modern life, is the ephemeral and the eternal Baudelaire spoke so often about, and identified at the beginning of *Le Peintre de la vie moderne* as the two constant elements of beauty. Baudelaire's *passante* is the powerful, concrete image of the ephemeral and the eternal as being constantly connected. She is the unknown, impersonal, "fugitive beauty" to which the poet addresses his everlasting question: "Will I ever see you again, but in eternity?"[86] But Barthes, in his Proustian mood, broke the spell of modernity, of modern art and criticism. As for Chateaubriand, for him, time is age, past memories, very well known people whom we have lost, our society that changed, our own body getting old. Unlike the poem or the fragment of the prose poem, the novel struggles to save a little bit of life from the devastation of time and asserts the existence of the past. Perhaps Barthes did not really want to write a novel, he just wanted to say that the novel, such a nineteenth-century object, so attacked by any avant-garde movement, is a beautiful literary form, filled with the charm of the past. And the great generality about the novel in the nineteenth century is that it aimed to reproduce reality, as photography did.

Photography gives us an undeniable certainty that a thing really existed in the past; it is the art of the *ça a été*. In photography, "the presence of the thing (at a certain past moment) is never metaphoric,"[87] just as life in animated beings is not metaphor but reality. But are we not perhaps too ready to confuse the real with the living? This confusion inhabits photography like a germ of insanity it can generate in the observer's mind, like the shadow of the mother whom Ulysses tried to embrace.

Two angles of vision therefore merge in the same concrete object, the photo of the winter garden. The first is the viewpoint of the essay, which seeks to define photography as the art of what has really existed; the second is the viewpoint of the novel, whose search is completely directed toward the mother and the truth of her being. From this union is born the third genre that Barthes speaks of in "Longtemps, je me suis couché de bonne heure." Produced by the fusion between novel and essay, it is a form as uncertain as the one that seduced Proust and Baudelaire, who both wrote in styles that borrowed from prose and poetry, from the essay and the novel. One can also understand from this union how the true argument of *Camera Lucida* is reality, exactly that reality that every literary work pursues and tries to represent, in spite of the inadequacy of language; a reality that is taken for granted in historical discourse.

Barthes's last book, his "note on photography," is none other than an analysis of the *reality effect* provoked by the photo of his mother as a child. Photography, the novel (or a third form), and history become superimposed forms in the race toward the real.

As in *Writing Degree Zero*, Barthes's history in *Camera Lucida* is not the discipline of historians, either the traditional or the new ones; it is a melancholic awareness of history and time devouring everything, every form and being. Barthes's questions about history end up in the consciousness of how close his generation is to the nineteenth century, since their parents were born at that time, the epoch of modernity. But the present world is so far away from the century that was haunted by historical research, founded history as the science of fact and the novel as the form representing reality, and invented photography. Disciplines, techniques, fields of knowledge disappear and are created anew. Everything changes, lapses away. Is memory really possible? Perhaps we are just about to die, and our recollections can only come from *outre-tombe*. Can we really remember today? We will see now, as a conclusion, that Proustian remembrance is not actually possible for Barthes, because longing for the past leads to hallucination.

Conclusion: The Return of History

Regarding the figure "Ravissement" in *A Lover's Discourse*, Barthes wrote, in parentheses, that "the being of photography is not to represent, but to cause remembrance." However, through the usual figure of inversion, the faculty of memory is denied in *Camera Lucida*: "Photography does not recall the past (nothing Proustian in a photograph). The effect it produces upon me is not to restore what has been abolished (by time, by distance), but to attest that what I see has indeed existed. Now, this is a strictly scandalous effect."[1]

These words indicated the most unexpected reversal to be found in the book and in Barthes himself—one ought not to forget that the *reversal* also points to the presence of the word "also" (the Princess Sherbatoff is *also* the madam of a brothel) and one ought to understand the term in its meaning of turning backward, as Orpheus turned backward, as the author of *Roland Barthes* does in speaking of a recession toward himself. In Barthes's most openly Proustian work one finds another author who seems to be a point of reference even more important than Proust: Michelet, the author one cannot identify with because of his ideology, but also the author that Barthes had studied as a critic, the author on whom Barthes had written the most— many articles and the 1954 book. Proust, the words and sentences of the *Recherche*, filtered into all of Barthes's writings. One can even say that they contain *Camera Lucida* in a kind of alliteration: Barthes's vision of art and life echoes Proust's. Michelet, on the other hand, emerges very seldom, with references that are few in number but very precise.

When Barthes denies that there is anything Proustian about photography, when he speaks of its scandalous effect, he is reaching the essential end point of Michelet and his history: resurrection. The effect or essence of photography is resurrection, the way that resurrection was the history of Michelet, who maintained that he had not reached the aim of history, only signaled it, calling it as no one before had ever called it: "Thierry saw a *narration* there and M. Guizot an *analysis*. I have called it *resurrection* and that name will remain with it."[2]

Resurrection has a hallucinatory character. It leads Michelet to search for the voice of the dead who make history; it leads Barthes to try to rediscover the presence, the being of his mother. But reality is absent, no longer living, like the dead of history. Paradoxically, photography does the same work that history (or rather historiography) does: it resuscitates the dead, because photography is the document of a reality that has existed, and history presents itself as documentary discourse, founded on the real and capable of reproducing it.

"A paradox," Barthes wrote in *Camera Lucida*, is that "the same century invented History and Photography."[3]

Barthes considered this paradoxical because photography succeeds in giving the evidence of the real, of the thing itself, whereas history only succeeds in signifying the real. The fundamental distrust of language inevitably returns: the difference between the sign and the thing. History would be on the side of the sign, and photography on the side of the thing. But a photo, like the image according to Blanchot,[4] embodies a lie. Barthes, overwhelmed with sorrow to the point of hallucination, is mistaken, because a photo, even if it gives us the undeniable certainty that the thing photographed really existed, does not give the thing back to us exactly. It gives us *almost* the thing itself: the thing minus the folly which would lead us to believe that the photo is the thing. But if one were to add in this madness, one would reach hallucination, and only hallucination can enable us to distinguish photography from history. One ought not to take this paradox too seriously, ought not to see it as a sign of a lack of coherence in Barthes's work. What else is paradox, the force of the term "paradoxically," which has guided my entire reading of Barthes, if not a circular syntax (the *also*), a figure of reversal or inversion, which abolishes logical contradiction in writing, and founds writing (and reading) on a continual oscillation and transformation? Circular syntax is a real alchemy or chemistry, which Michelet found so seductive and which is at the foundation of photographic technique.

The image of photography had already appeared in Barthes's article "Michelet, l'Histoire et la Mort" (1952): "Thus the flesh of men who follow each other preserves the obscure trace of the incidents of History, until the day when the historian, like a photographer, *reveals* through a chemical operation that which has previously been experienced."[5]

History inevitably reappears for the same reason that Barthes understood the *noema* of photography by looking at a photo of his mother as a child he never knew; and

Barthes maintained that history is nothing other than the time before we were born: "That is what the time when my mother was alive *before me* is—History (moreover, it is the period which interests me most, historically)."[6]

The real that photography renders authentic is, however, absent: constitutionally a photograph has something in common with a cadaver. Death is inherent in it, all the more so when it is the image of a loved one who is now dead: a real theater of death, and a dead theater, because it is immobilized in time. The resurrection that is operated by photography, again in contrast to Proustian memory, implies a double death, not only because it shows someone who is dead, but also because the resurrection is brief: in the end, after a moment of recognition, it is nothing but a flat, fleeting image, as light as the paper it is made of, as violently concrete as a small fragile object, because it fills our vision, violent as the modern objects of Robbe-Grillet.

One can do nothing with photography except watch it pass. One cannot make it more profound; one can only describe it. In *Roland Barthes*, Barthes spoke in similar terms of the voice, that bizarre thing which one *reremembers* fugitively in the ear. One looks in vain for words that can accurately express the quality of a voice, because "a voice is always *already* dead, and it is by a kind of desperate denial that we call it: living; this irremediable loss we give the name of *inflection:* inflection is the voice insofar as it is always past, silenced."[7] Description can only have a funereal quality. In his last book, Barthes is describing. He is not only describing the path taken by his intellectual research when he sought to understand photography, but also describing, without showing it, the photo of the winter garden: his mother who was five years old, her hands, the expression on her face, the clarity of her eyes.

Photograph and voice are the opposites of memory, of Monument, because they are fugitive, because we describe them without being able to deepen them: they are the light and destructible materiality of oblivion. They require the superhuman force of a Sisyphus because we can say so little about them.

But photography is a historical object, the same one that signaled the beginning of modernity, our renunciation of the Monument, our inability to conceive of duration symbolically. At the most lacerating moment of suffering, of the *punctum*, photography presents itself as a historical object, which is what literature was in *Writing Degree Zero*. It can only be the sign of its own historicity, beyond its historical opacity and superficiality; it touches something in the deep history of our time, in the way in which our society, rejecting all rites, takes on the image of death, of a nonsymbolic death, and falls abruptly "into literal Death."[8]

Photography joins literature, of which Barthes wrote in his *Critical Essays:* "Is not literature, that particular language which makes the 'subject' into the sign of history?"[9] Since, as Barthes said in *Writing Degree Zero*, history acts most clearly when it has been rejected, the statement made in *Camera Lucida*, "I am the very contrary of History,"[10] is to be understood as a sign of history, as its completely deadly and funereal component, so close to Michelet's history. Barthes thought he was writing that third form between the essay and the novel, a novel about the person he loved, a work that would tear her from oblivion and from history which engulfs all beings and time; he ended up writing about history once more. And in a way that is close to Michelet, to his unbearable romantic *pathos*, since Barthes's history cannot be accepted by historians exactly because it is a lyrical and moral history, like Michelet's: "This is a laceration so intense, so intolerable that, alone against his century, Michelet conceived of History as a love's Protest: to perpetuate not only life but also what he called, in his vocabulary so outdated today, the Good, Justice, Unity, etc."[11]

Notes

Introduction

1. Barthes, "Inaugural Lecture, Collège de France," *A Barthes Reader* p. 478 (p. 46). I cite English translations when they are available. The page reference of the original, in parentheses, follows that of the translation.

2. Blanchot, "Rousseau," *Le Livre à venir*, p. 69 (my translation).

1 History and Form

1. Lavers, *Roland Barthes: Structuralism and After*, p. 51. Lavers points out the influence of Saussure through Merleau-Ponty and Sartre, who, in the early 1940s, used some Saussurian terminology without mentioning the Swiss linguist.

2. Ungar, *Roland Barthes: The Professor of Desire*, p. 9.

3. "The work, method, spirit of Lanson, himself a prototype of the French professor, has controlled, through countless epigones, the whole of academic criticism for fifty years" (Barthes, "What Is Criticism?" *Critical Essays*, p. 256 [p. 253]). Antoine Compagnon, who studied with Barthes, has recently published a study on Gustave Lanson and Lansonism: *La Troisième République des lettres, de Flaubert à Proust*.

4. Barthes obtained his *licence* in classics at the Sorbonne in 1939, taught at the *Lycée* in Biarritz and in Paris for two years, and from 1941 to 1947

suffered from tuberculosis. After a convalescence in Paris, when he published in *Combat*, he became assistant librarian and then professor at the Institut français of Bucharest (Rumania) in 1948–49 and reader at the University of Alexandria (Egypt) in 1949–50. He then worked in Paris from 1950 to 1952, at the Direction générale des relations culturelles of the Ministère des affaires étrangères, before joining the CNRS (Centre national de la recherche scientifique) from 1952 to 1954.

5. Benjamin, "The Author as Producer," *Reflections*, p. 222.

6. Barthes, *Writing Degree Zero*, p. 13 (p. 14).

7. Barthes, "Literature Today," *Critical Essays*, p. 151 (p. 155).

8. Benjamin, "Author as Producer," *Reflections*, p. 235.

9. As mentioned by Roger, *Roland Barthes, roman*, p. 318.

10. See Barthes, *Roland Barthes*, p. 145 (p. 148).

11. Ungar, *Roland Barthes*, p. 10.

12. Roger, *Roland Barthes*, p. 252 (my translation).

13. Barthes, *Writing Degree Zero*, pp. 16–17 (p. 16).

14. Ibid., p. 18 (p. 17).

15. Ibid., p. 9 (p. 11).

16. Sontag, Preface to Barthes, *Writing Degree Zero*, p. x.

17. Ungar, *Roland Barthes*, p. 13.

18. Flaubert, *The Letters of Gustave Flaubert* (1830–1857), p. 154 (*Œuvres complètes: Correspondance* 2:343–44).

19. Roger, *Roland Barthes*, p. 246 (my translation).

20. Such is the title Ungar gives to one of his book's last chapters, which deals with *Camera Lucida* and Barthes's link to Proust (*Roland Barthes*, pp. 135–51).

21. See Barthes, "Interview: A Conversation with Roland Barthes," *The Grain of the Voice: Interviews, 1962–1980*, p. 140 (p. 133). This text is cited by Ungar, *Roland Barthes*, p. 14.

22. Barthes, *Writing Degree Zero*, p. 2 (p. 7).

23. Ibid., p. 17 (p. 17).

24. Ibid., p. 2 (p. 7).

25. See Sartre, *Qu'est-ce que la littérature?* pp. 63–70. Sontag talks about Sartre's naive conception of form: see her preface to Barthes, *Writing Degree Zero*, p. xii.

26. Barthes, *Writing Degree Zero*, pp. 4–5 (p. 9).

27. See Lanson, "L'Esprit scientifique et la méthode de l'histoire littéraire," *Méthodes de l'histoire littéraire*, pp. 21–22.

28. See Foucault, *Histoire de la folie à l'âge classique*, p. 13.

29. A typical example of allegory can be found in these lines of Boileau's *L'Art poétique*, where he praises a flourished style: "J'aime mieux un ruisseau qui, sur la molle arène, / Dans un pré plein de fleurs lentement se promène, / Qu'un torrent débordé qui, d'un cours orageux, / Roule plein de gravier sur un terrain fangeux." See Fontanier, *Les Figures du discours*, p. 115.

30. Barthes, *Writing Degree Zero*, pp. 87–88 (p. 64).

31. Ibid., p. 28 (p. 24).

32. Ibid., p. 88 (p. 64).

33. Cited by Roger, *Roland Barthes*, p. 260 (my translation).

34. Barthes, *Roland Barthes*, p. 53 (p. 57).

35. Roger, *Roland Barthes*, p. 261.

36. Barthes's "Culture et tragédie" was first published as "Essais sur la culture," *Cahiers de l'étudiant* (Special issue, Spring 1942), and was partially republished in *Le Monde*, 4 April 1986, p. 19. See Roger, *Roland Barthes*, p. 334.

37. Lavers believes that "it may well be in the tension between the collective and the individual that the key to Barthes can best be found" (*Roland Barthes*, p. 3).

38. Blanchot, "The Future and the Question of Art," *The Space of Literature*, p. 213 (p. 284). Roger maintains that *"Writing Degree Zero* is closer to Blanchot than to Sartre. One should even go further, and say that this book is more Blanchot than Blanchot himself, who, strangely enough, will consider in his review excessive the privilege given by Barthes to form" (*Roland Barthes*, pp. 248–49 [my translation]).

39. Todorov, *Critique de la critique: Un Roman d'apprentissage*, pp. 74–81.

40. Barthes, *Writing Degree Zero*, p. 12 (p. 13).

41. Blanchot, "La Recherche du point zéro," *Le Livre à venir*, p. 301.

42. Discussing Baudelaire and Poe, Benjamin talks about "the shock experience which the passer-by has in the crowd" ("On Some Motifs in Baudelaire," *Illuminations*, p. 176).

43. Hofmannsthal, *The Letter of Lord Chandos*, *Selected Prose*, p. 140.

44. Ibid., pp. 134–35. This same passage is cited by Blanchot in "Inspiration, Lack of Inspiration," *Space of Literature*, p. 183 (p. 244).

45. See Sartre, *Qu'est-ce que la littérature?* pp. 64–65. Sartre distinguishes the poet, who treats words as objects, from the writer in prose, for whom words are significations.

46. Barthes, *Writing Degree Zero*, p. 47 (p. 37).

47. Ibid., pp. 75–76 (p. 55).

48. Benjamin, *Briefe* 2:852 (my translation).

49. Barthes, *Roland Barthes*, p. 92 (p. 96).

50. Barthes, "Deliberation," *The Rustle of Language*, p. 367 (p. 408). Roger perceives Barthes as juggling with modernity and tradition, with the avant-garde and classicism: he can at the same time declare that he is classical and that he is close to his friends of *Tel Quel* (see *Roland Barthes*, pp. 238–39).

51. Baudelaire, *Le Peintre de la vie moderne*, *Œuvres complètes* 2:695 (my translation).

52. Barthes, "Culture et tragédie," *Le Monde*, 4 April 1986, p. 19.

53. Hofmannsthal, "Die Bühne als Traumbild," *Prosa* 2:64 (my translation).

54. See Hofmannsthal, "Der Dichter und seine Zeit," *Prosa* 2:229–58, and Blanchot, "Inspiration," *Space of Literature*, p. 180 (p. 239).

55. Barthes, "Culture et tragédie," *Le Monde*, 4 April 1986, p. 19 (my translation).

56. Barthes, *Roland Barthes*, p. 92 (p. 96).

57. See Tzvetan Todorov, "La Réflexion sur la littérature dans la France contemporaine," *Poétique* 38 (1979): 131–48. Todorov considers Barthes and Blanchot the romantics of today.

58. Barthes, *Writing Degree Zero*, p. 82 (p. 60).

59. Ibid., pp. 62–63 (p. 46).

60. Barthes, *Roland Barthes*, p. 180 (p. 182).

61. See Camus, *Le Mythe de Sisyphe, Essais*, p. 101.

62. Barthes, *Michelet*, p. 18 (p. 18).

63. Hofmannsthal, "Colours. From the *Letters of a Man Who Returned*," *Selected Prose*, p. 148; *Die Briefe des Zurückgekerten*, *Prosa* 2:306.

64. Blanchot, "Inspiration," *Space of Literature*, p. 181 (p. 241).

65. Hofmannsthal, "Colours," *Selected Prose*, p. 153.

66. Ungar, *Roland Barthes*, p. 15.

67. Barthes, "Michelet's Modernity," *Rustle of Language*, p. 208 (p. 239).

68. Ibid., p. 211 (p. 242).

69. See Barthes, "Michelet, Today," *Rustle of Language*, p. 197 (p. 227).

70. Nietzsche, *Götzen-Dämmerung*, p. 105 (my translation).

71. Regarding Van Gogh and the overturning of perspective, see Meyer

Shapiro, "On a Painting of Van Gogh (*Crows over the Wheat Field*)," *View* 1 (Fall 1946): 8–13, reprinted in Shapiro, *Modern Art, Nineteenth and Twentieth Centuries: Selected Papers*, pp. 87–99.

72. Barthes, *Michelet*, p. 3 (p. 5).

73. Barthes, *Writing Degree Zero*, pp. 10–11 (p. 12).

74. Barthes, *Michelet*, p. 18 (pp. 17–18).

75. Barthes, "Inaugural Lecture," *Barthes Reader*, p. 467 (pp. 25–26).

76. Richard, *Poésie et profondeur*, p. 10 (my translation).

77. Barthes, *A Lover's Discourse*, p. 4 (p. 8).

78. See Barthes, "The Death of the Author," *Rustle of Language*, pp. 49–55 (pp. 61–67), and Foucault, "Qu'est-ce qu'un auteur?" *Bulletin de la Société française de philosophie* 3 (July–September 1969), pp. 73–104.

79. Barthes, "Michelet, l'Histoire et la Mort," *Esprit* 178 (April 1951): 503 (my translation).

80. Barthes, "La Sorcière," *Critical Essays*, p. 103 (p. 112).

81. Barthes, "A Great Rhetorician of Erotic Figures," *Grain of the Voice*, p. 253 (p. 239). This corresponds to what Barthes called "the last point in Febvre's program: what we might call the phenomena of collective mentality" ("History or Literature?" *On Racine*, p. 160 [p. 154]).

82. Barthes, "History or Literature?" *On Racine*, p. 156 (p. 151).

83. Febvre, "La Sensibilité et l'histoire: Comment reconstituer la vie affective d'autrefois?" p. 13 (my translation).

84. Ibid., p. 18.

85. See Barthes, "Structural Analysis of Narratives," *Barthes Reader*, pp. 251–95 ("Introduction à l'analyse structurale des récits," *Communications* 8:1966, pp. 1–27).

86. Barthes, "The Discourse of History," *Rustle of Language*, p. 138 (p. 164).

87. Veyne, *L'Inventaire des différences: Leçon inaugurale au Collège de France*, p. 48.

2 Against Language

1. Barthes, "The Structuralist Activity," *Critical Essays*, pp. 219–20 (pp. 219–20).

2. See Gadamer, *Truth and Method*, and Habermas, *Legitimation Crisis*. On rhetoric, see Vattimo, *La fine della modernità*, especially chapter 8, "Verità e retorica nell'ontologia ermeneutica," pp. 138–52, in which rhetoric is understood in the broader sense as the art of persuasion which

upholds the truth of verisimilitude as opposed to truth founded on certainty—supposed certainty—and demonstration typical of science. This difference seems particularly important to me because it takes us back to the difference between literature and science that Barthes later individuated and that I discuss in the last chapter of this book. On the ends of persuasion, see Antoine Compagnon, "Sur la légitimité du discours politique (la persuasion de la persuasion)," *Critique* 401 (October 1980): 925–47. On the valorization of rhetoric, see Perelman and Olbrechts-Tyteca, *The New Rhetoric: A Treatise on Argumentation*.

3. Barthes, "The Image," *Rustle of Language*, pp. 350–51 (pp. 389–90). In spite of this, Barthes was interested in rhetoric and heralded the modern study of ancient rhetoric: "We have no modern work on classical rhetoric; generally the figures of thought are relegated to a museum of pedantic formalism, as if they had existed only in a few treatises by Jesuit fathers" (Barthes, "History or Literature?" *On Racine*, p. 160 [pp. 154–55]). See also Barthes, "L'ancienne rhétorique," *Communications* 16 (1970), pp. 172–229.

4. See Lacan, *Écrits*, especially "Le Séminaire sur 'La Lettre volée,'" pp. 11–64, and "L'Instance de la lettre dans l'inconscient ou la raison depuis Freud," pp. 493–530.

5. Derrida, *Of Grammatology*, p. 3 (p. 11).

6. Ibid., pp. 11–12 (pp. 22–23).

7. See Foucault, *Surveiller et punir*, pp. 122–29, on the prison as a mechanism of knowledge, and pp. 194–96, on power as producer of reality. See also the well-known debate between Foucault and Derrida on Descartes's *Meditations:* Foucault, "Mon Corps, ce papier, ce feu," *Histoire de la folie*, pp. 583–603.

8. See Roger, *Roland Barthes*, pp. 18–19.

9. Barthes, *Roland Barthes*, p. 115 (pp. 118–19).

10. Barthes, *Writing Degree Zero*, p. 19 (p. 18).

11. Barthes, "A Magnificent Gift," *Rustle of Language*, p. 159 (p. 187).

12. See Derrida's discussion of Saussure, *Grammatology*, chapter 2, "Linguistics and Grammatology," pp. 27–73 (pp. 42–108) and especially pp. 38–42 (pp. 57–62).

13. See Starobinski, *Les Mots sous les mots: Les Anagrammes de Ferdinand de Saussure*.

14. Barthes, "Magnificent Gift," *Rustle of Language*, p. 159 (p. 187).

15. Genette, "L'Envers des signes," *Figures I*, pp. 195–96 (my translation).

16. See Barthes, "Myth Today," *Mythologies*, p. 116 (p. 201). See also Heath's analysis of the same example: *Vertige du déplacement: Lecture de Barthes*, pp. 44–45.

17. Barthes, "Myth Today," *Mythologies*, p. 134 (p. 221).

18. Genette, "L'Envers des signes," *Figures I*, p. 202 (my translation).

19. Barthes, "Inaugural Lecture," *Barthes Reader*, p. 476 (p. 41).

20. Barthes, *Roland Barthes*, p. 161 (p. 164).

21. Barthes, "From Work to Text," *Rustle of Language*, p. 57 (pp. 70–71).

22. Ibid., p. 64 (p. 77). All of *The Pleasure of the Text* treats this theme.

23. Barthes, *Sade, Fourier, Loyola*, p. 3 (p. 8).

24. "The amorous subject experiences every meeting with the loved being as a festival" (Barthes, *A Lover's Discourse: Fragments*, p. 119 [p. 139]).

25. Barthes, *Sade, Fourier, Loyola*, p. 6 (pp. 10–11).

26. Ibid., p. 6 (p. 11).

27. On the theme of obstinacy, see Antoine Compagnon, "L'Entêtement d'écrire," *Critique* 423–24 (August–September 1982): 666–80.

28. Barthes, "Style and Its Image," *Rustle of Language*, p. 90 (p. 141).

29. Ibid., p. 91 (p. 142).

30. Ibid., p. 94 (p. 145).

31. Cf. Barthes, "Writers, Intellectuals, Teachers," *Rustle of Language*, pp. 309–31 (pp. 345–68).

32. Barthes, *Pleasure of the Text*, pp. 3–4 (p. 10).

33. Blanchot, *La Folie du jour*, p. 29 (my translation).

34. Ibid., p. 31 (my translation).

35. Barthes, "Of What Use an Intellectual?" *Grain of the Voice*, p. 261 (p. 247).

36. Barthes, *Sade, Fourier, Loyola*, p. 7 (p. 12).

37. Ibid., p. 8 (p. 13).

38. Ibid., p. 7 (p. 12).

39. Barthes, *Roland Barthes*, p. 43 (p. 47).

40. Barthes, *Pleasure of the Text*, p. 66 (p. 104).

41. Ibid., p. 24 (p. 42).

42. Ibid., pp. 15–16 (p. 28).

43. Ibid., p. 66 (p. 105).

44. Ibid., pp. 66–67 (p. 105).

45. Ibid., p. 66 (p. 104).

46. Barthes, *Michelet*, p. 81 (p. 73).

47. Barthes, *Pleasure of the Text*, p. 67 (p. 105).

48. Barthes, "Style and Its Image," *Rustle of Language*, p. 96 (p. 147).

49. See Benveniste, "La Nature des pronoms" and "De la subjectivité dans le langage," *Problèmes de linguistique générale* 1:251–57, 258–76.

50. Barthes, "Why I Love Benveniste," *Rustle of Language*, p. 164 (p. 193).

51. Barthes, *Pleasure of the Text*, p. 67 (p. 105).

52. Lavers, *Roland Barthes*, p. 206.

53. Roger, *Roland Barthes*, p. 339 (my translation).

54. Barthes, *Roland Barthes*, p. 107 (p. 111).

55. Barthes, *Incidents*, p. 35 (my translation).

56. Barthes, *Roland Barthes*, p. 99 (p. 103). Roger insists on the Gidian component of Barthes: see *Roland Barthes*, pp. 16, 314–17.

57. Lavers, *Roland Barthes*, p. 208.

58. Barthes, *Pleasure of the Text*, pp. 55–56 (pp. 88–89).

59. Ibid., p. 4 (p. 11).

60. Barthes, *Mythologies*, p. 64, quoted by Genette, "L'Envers des signes," *Figures I*, p. 201.

61. Barthes, *Roland Barthes*, p. 102 (p. 106).

62. Blanchot, *Le Pas au-delà*, p. 102 (my translation).

63. Barthes, *Pleasure of the Text*, p. 23 (p. 39).

64. Barthes, *Lover's Discourse*, p. 116 (p. 133).

65. Barthes, "The Image," *Rustle of Language*, p. 351 (p. 390).

66. Ibid., p. 357 (p. 396).

67. Barthes, *Roland Barthes*, p. 89 (p. 93).

68. Roger, *Roland Barthes*, p. 22 (my translation).

69. Barthes, "Literature Today," *Critical Essays*, p. 154 (p. 157).

70. Genette, "L'Envers des signes," *Figures I*, p. 204 (my translation).

71. Barthes, "Literature and Signification," *Critical Essays*, p. 268 (p. 265).

72. Blanchot, "The Gaze of Orpheus," *"The Gaze of Orpheus," and Other Literary Essays*, p. 99 ("Le Regard d'Orphée," *L'Espace littéraire*, p. 227). On the theme of Orpheus in Blanchot, see Giovanni Vattimo, "L'essenza mortale della letteratura," *Sigma* 16 (1983): 61–66. See also Giorgio Patrizi, "Blanchot o la volontà di letteratura," *Lectures* 10 (June 1982): 129–42, and, on Barthes, Roland A. Champagne, "Between Orpheus and Eurydice: Barthes and the Historicity of Reading," *Clio* 7 (1978–79): 229–38.

73. Blanchot, "Gaze of Orpheus," *"Gaze of Orpheus,"* p. 99 ("Le Regard d'Orphée," *L'Espace littéraire*, p. 227).

74. Ibid.

75. Barthes, *Roland Barthes*, p. 179 (p. 181). Barthes wrote a foreword to "La Rochefoucauld: *Reflections or Sentences and Maximes*," *New Critical Essays*, pp. 3–22 (*"Le Degré zéro de l'écriture," suivi des "Nouveaux Essais critiques,"* pp. 69–88).

76. Ibid., p. 94 (p. 97).

77. Blanchot, "The Original Experience," *Space of Literature*, p. 236 (p. 320).

78. See Blanchot, "La Folie par excellence," foreword to Jaspers, *Strindberg et Van Gogh, Hölderlin et Swedenborg*, pp. 9–33.

79. Blanchot, "Gaze of Orpheus," *"Gaze of Orpheus,"* p. 102 ("Le Regard d'Orphée," *L'Espace littéraire*, p. 232).

80. Blanchot, "The Essential Solitude," *"Gaze of Orpheus,"* pp. 72–73 ("La Solitude essentielle," *L'Espace littéraire*, p. 22).

81. Barthes, "Digressions," *Le Bruissement de la langue: Essais critiques IV*, p. 85 (my translation).

82. Ibid., p. 86.

83. Ibid.

84. Blanchot, "L'Échec du démon: La Vocation," *Le Livre à venir*, p. 123 (my translation).

85. See Roger, *Roland Barthes*, p. 30.

86. See Blanchot, "La Parole prophétique," *Le Livre à venir*, p. 118.

87. Blanchot, "L'Avenir et la question de l'art," *L'Espace littéraire*, p. 288 (my translation).

88. Blanchot, "Rilke and Death's Demand," *Space of Literature*, p. 158 (pp. 209–10).

89. See Lacan, "Le Stade du miroir comme formateur de la fonction du Je," *Écrits*, pp. 93–100.

90. Barthes, *Lover's Discourse*, p. 141 (p. 168).

91. Barthes, *Critical Essays*, p. xi (p. 9).

92. This struggle against the constitutional conformism of language was also Henri Beyle's struggle. See Michel Crouzet, *Stendhal et le langage*, especially chapters 1 and 2, pp. 11–80.

93. Barthes, "Music, Voice, Language," *The Responsibility of Forms: New Critical Essays on Music, Art, and Representation*, p. 281 (p. 249).

94. Barthes, "Outcomes of the Text," *Rustle of Language*, p. 238 (p. 271). On classical reminiscences in Barthes, see Claude Reichler, "L'Ombre," *Critique* 423–24 (August–September 1982): 767–74.

95. Barthes, "Inaugural Lecture," *Barthes Reader*, p. 476 (p. 41).

96. Proust, *Remembrance of Things Past* 3:931 (3:895).

97. Ibid.

3 Essays in Fiction

1. Barthes, "Literature and Signification," *Critical Essays*, p. 268 (p. 265).

2. Barthes, "Inaugural Lecture," *Barthes Reader*, p. 463 (p. 18).

3. Barthes, *Camera Lucida: Reflections on Photography*, p. 97 (p. 151).

4. Barthes, "Literature Today," *Critical Essays*, p. 159 (p. 163).

5. Ibid., p. 160 (p. 164).

6. Lacan, "Fonction et champ de la parole et du language," *Écrits*, p. 276 (my translation).

7. Barthes, "Taking Sides," *Critical Essays*, p. 164 (p. 168).

8. Barthes, "Objective Literature," *Critical Essays*, p. 14 (p. 30).

9. Ibid., p. 16 (p. 32).

10. Barthes, "Literal Literature," *Critical Essays*, p. 55 (p. 67).

11. Barthes, "Objective Literature," *Critical Essays*, p. 24 (p. 40).

12. Blanchot, "The Clarity of Fiction," *The Sirens' Song: Selected Essays*, p. 209 ("La Clarté romanesque," *Le Livre à venir*, p. 239).

13. Ibid., p. 208 (p. 237).

14. Ibid., p. 210 (p. 240).

15. Ibid., p. 211 (p. 243).

16. Barthes, "The Last Word on Robbe-Grillet?" *Critical Essays*, p. 203 (p. 204).

17. Barthes, "Discourse of History," *Rustle of Language*, p. 138 (p. 164).

18. Ibid., p. 139 (p. 165).

19. Barthes, "The Reality Effect," *Rustle of Language*, p. 148 (p. 174). On the reality effect and literary realism which goes beyond Barthes's too schematic vision between the *parce que* (discourse typical of realism) and the *pour que* (requirement of discourse itself), see Michel Crouzet, "Une Rhétorique de Maupassant," *Revue d'histoire littéraire de la France* 2 (March–April 1980): 233–61.

20. Barthes, "Taking Sides," *Critical Essays*, p. 170 (p. 174).

21. Barthes, "Literature and Metalanguage," *Critical Essays*, p. 99 (p. 106).

22. Barthes, "Taking Sides," *Critical Essays*, p. 170 (p. 174).

23. This is the reading of Loris that is proposed by Massimo Cacciari in "Intransitabili utopie," postface to Hofmannsthal, *La Torre*, trans. Silvia Bortoli (Milan: Adelphi, 1978), pp. 157–216.

24. Barthes, "Inaugural Lecture," *Barthes Reader*, p. 465 (p. 21).

25. Ibid.

26. Barthes, "Longtemps, je me suis couché de bonne heure," *Rustle of Language*, p. 287 (p. 322).

27. Barthes, "Inaugural Lecture," *Barthes Reader*, p. 461 (p. 14).

28. Sontag, "Writing Itself: On Roland Barthes," introduction to *Barthes Reader*, p. xxii.

29. Barthes, *Roland Barthes*, p. 88 (p. 92).

30. Barthes, "Inaugural Lecture," *Barthes Reader*, p. 458 (p. 9).

31. Ibid., p. 459 (pp. 10–11).

32. See Blanchot, "Il ne saurait pas être question de bien finir," *Le Livre à venir*, pp. 50–51. Blanchot distinguishes between "the language in the world" which is power and "the language without power in the literary work."

33. Barthes wrote an essay on Queneau: "Zazie and Literature," *Critical Essays*, pp. 117–24 (pp. 125–33).

34. Barthes, "Inaugural Lecture," *Barthes Reader*, p. 466 (p. 23).

35. Ibid., p. 466 (p. 25).

36. Ibid., p. 467 (p. 26).

37. Barthes, *Critique et vérité*, p. 57 (my translation).

38. Barthes, "Death of the Author," *Rustle of Language*, p. 55 (p. 67).

39. Barthes, "From Science to Literature," *Rustle of Language*, p. 5 (p. 15).

40. Ibid., p. 8 (p. 18).

41. Ibid., p. 10 (p. 20).

42. Ibid.

43. Barthes, "Inaugural Lecture," *Barthes Reader*, p. 464 (p. 20).

44. Barthes often wrote about cooking. See, for example, his "Reading Brillat-Savarin," *Rustle of Language*, pp. 250–70 (pp. 285–306).

45. Barthes, "Inaugural Lecture," *Barthes Reader*, p. 464 (p. 21).

46. Ibid.

47. Barthes, "Outcomes of the Text," *Rustle of Language*, p. 247 (p. 280).

48. Barthes, "The Image," *Rustle of Language*, p. 357 (p. 396).

49. Barthes, "Deliberation," *Rustle of Language*, p. 367 (p. 407).

50. Barthes, "Inaugural Lecture," *Barthes Reader*, p. 470 (p. 31).

51. Ibid., p. 470 (pp. 31–32).

52. Lanson, "L'Esprit scientifique," *Méthodes de l'histoire littéraire*, p. 30 (my translation).

53. Hofmannsthal, *The Letter of Lord Chandos, Selected Prose*, p. 138.

54. Proust, "Projets de préface," *Contre Sainte-Beuve*, p. 211 (my translation). These pages of criticism then became the very text of the *Recherche*.

55. Proust, *Time Regained, Remembrance of Things Past* 3:935 (3:898).

56. Ricoeur, *Temps et récit* 2:194–225.

57. Proust, *Contre Sainte-Beuve*, p. 557 (my translation).

58. Barthes, "An Idea of Research," *Rustle of Language*, p. 272 (p. 308).

59. Barthes, *Pleasure of the Text*, p. 36 (p. 59).

60. Barthes, "Longtemps," *Rustle of Language*, p. 289 (p. 325).

61. Barthes, "An Idea of Research," *Rustle of Language*, p. 275 (p. 311).

62. Barthes, "Longtemps," *Rustle of Language*, p. 285 (pp. 320–21).

63. Proust, *Remembrance of Things Past* 3:973–74 (3:932).

64. Barthes, "Chateaubriand: *Life of Rancé*," *New Critical Essays*, p. 42 (p. 108).

65. Barthes, "An Idea of Research," *Rustle of Language*, p. 275 (p. 311).

66. Proust, *Remembrance of Things Past* 3:931 (3:895).

67. Ibid. 3:932 (3:896).

68. Barthes, "Longtemps," *Rustle of Language*, p. 277 (p. 313).

69. Barthes, "Literature and Signification," *Critical Essays*, p. 275 (p. 272).

70. Proust, *Remembrance of Things Past* 3:932 (3:896).

71. Barthes, *Roland Barthes*, p. 90 (p. 94).

72. Proust, *Remembrance of Things Past* 3:1095 (3:1038).

73. Barthes, "Longtemps," *Rustle of Language*, p. 290 (p. 325).

74. Barthes, " Taking Sides," *Critical Essays*, p. 170 (p. 174).

75. Barthes, "Longtemps," *Rustle of Language*, p. 290 (p. 325).

76. Ibid., p. 289 (p. 325).

77. Proust, *Contre Sainte-Beuve*, p. 645 (my translation).

78. Barthes, "Why I Love Benveniste," *Rustle of Language*, p. 164 (p. 193).

79. See Barthes, *Lover's Discourse*, pp. 75–79 (pp. 89–94).

80. Barthes, "Longtemps," *Rustle of Language*, pp. 285–86 (p. 321).

81. Barthes, "Chateaubriand," *New Critical Essays*, p. 44 (p. 109).

82. See Barthes, *Incidents*, p. 76.

83. Proust, *Remembrance of Things Past* 3:937 (3:900).

84. Barthes, *Camera Lucida*, p. 75 (p. 117).

85. Barthes, "Longtemps," *Rustle of Language*, p. 289 (p. 324).

86. Baudelaire, "A une passante," *Les Fleurs du mal*, *Œuvres complètes* 1:93 (my translation).

87. Barthes, *Camera Lucida*, p. 78 (p. 123). See Éric Marty, "L'Assomption du phénomène," and Chantal Thomas, "La Photo du jardin d'hiver," *Critique* 423–24 (August–September 1982): 744–52 and 797–804 respectively.

Conclusion: The Return of History

1. Barthes, *Camera Lucida*, p. 82 (p. 129).

2. Michelet, *Le Peuple*, p. 146 (my translation).

3. Barthes, *Camera Lucida*, p. 93 (p. 146).

4. See Blanchot, "Les Deux Versions de l'imaginaire," *L'Espace littéraire*, p. 344. Barthes cites this essay in *Camera Lucida*, p. 106. Blanchot's essay was certainly important for the whole conception of the second part of *Camera Lucida*, since it argues that the image has something in common with the cadaver.

5. Barthes, "Michelet, l'Histoire et la Mort," *Esprit* 178 (April 1951): 509.

6. Barthes, *Camera Lucida*, p. 65 (p. 102). Moreover, this era coincides with Proust's.

7. Barthes, *Roland Barthes*, p. 68 (p. 72).

8. Barthes, *Camera Lucida*, p. 92 (p. 144).

9. Barthes, "Literature Today," *Critical Essays*, p. 161 (p. 166).

10. Barthes, *Camera Lucida*, p. 65 (p. 102).

11. Ibid., p. 94 (p. 147).

Bibliography

The following lists include only works I cite in this book. Whenever possible, I have supplied available English translations for works originally published in French or German. Comprehensive bibliographies on Roland Barthes can be found in the books by Stephen Heath, Annette Lavers, and Steven Ungar (listed below under "Books and Special Issues on Roland Barthes").

Books by Roland Barthes

Le Degré zéro de l'écriture. Paris: Seuil, "Pierres vives," 1953. Reprint, with *Nouveaux Essais critiques*. Paris: Seuil, "Points," 1972. *Writing Degree Zero*. Translated by Annette Lavers and Colin Smith; preface by Susan Sontag. New York: Hill and Wang, 1968. *New Critical Essays*. Translated by Richard Howard. New York: Hill and Wang, 1980.

Michelet par lui-même. Paris: Seuil, "Écrivains de toujours," 1954. *Michelet*. Translated by Richard Howard. New York: Hill and Wang, 1987.

Mythologies. Paris: Seuil, "Pierres vives," 1957. Reprint. Paris: Seuil, "Points," 1970. *Mythologies*. Selected and translated by Annette Lavers. New York: Hill and Wang, 1972. *The Eiffel Tower and Other Mythologies*. Translated by Richard Howard. New York: Hill and Wang, 1979.

Sur Racine. Paris: Seuil, "Pierres vives," 1963. Reprint. Paris: Seuil,

"Points," 1980. *On Racine.* Translated by Richard Howard. New York: Hill and Wang, 1964.

Essais critiques. Paris: Seuil, "Tel Quel," 1964. Reprint. Paris: Seuil, "Points," 1981. *Critical Essays.* Translated by Richard Howard. Evanston, Ill.: Northwestern University Press, 1972.

Critique et vérité. Paris: Seuil, "Tel Quel," 1966. *Criticism and Truth.* Translated by Katrine Pilcher Keuneman; foreword by Philip Thody. London: Athlone Press, 1987.

Système de la mode. Paris: Seuil, 1967. *The Fashion System.* Translated by Matthew Ward and Richard Howard. New York: Hill and Wang, 1983.

S/Z. Paris: Seuil, "Tel Quel," 1970. Reprint. Paris: Seuil, "Points," 1976. *S/Z.* Translated by Richard Miller. New York: Hill and Wang, 1974.

Sade, Fourier, Loyola. Paris: Seuil, "Tel Quel," 1971. *Sade, Fourier, Loyola.* Translated by Richard Miller. New York: Hill and Wang, 1976.

Le Plaisir du texte. Paris: Seuil, "Tel Quel," 1973. Reprint. Paris: Seuil, "Points," 1981. *The Pleasure of the Text.* Translated by Richard Miller. New York: Hill and Wang, 1975.

Roland Barthes. Paris: Seuil, "Écrivains de toujours," 1975. *Roland Barthes.* Translated by Richard Howard. New York: Hill and Wang, 1977.

Fragments d'un discours amoureux. Paris: Seuil, "Tel Quel," 1977. *A Lover's Discourse: Fragments.* Translated by Richard Howard. New York: Hill and Wang, 1978.

Leçon. Paris: Seuil, 1978. "Inaugural Lecture, Collège de France." Translated by Richard Howard. In *A Barthes Reader,* edited, with an introduction, by Susan Sontag. New York: Hill and Wang, 1982.

La Chambre claire: Note sur la photographie. Paris: Seuil/Gallimard, "Cahiers du cinéma," 1980. *Camera Lucida: Reflections on Photography.* Translated by Richard Howard. New York: Hill and Wang, 1981.

Le Grain de la voix: Entretiens, 1962–1980. Paris: Seuil, 1981. *The Grain of the Voice: Interviews, 1962–1980.* Translated by Linda Coverdale. New York: Hill and Wang, 1984.

L'Obvie et l'obtus: Essais critiques III. Paris: Seuil, 1982. *The Responsibility of Forms: New Critical Essays on Music, Art, and Representation.* Translated by Richard Howard. New York: Hill and Wang, 1984.

Le Bruissement de la langue: Essais critiques IV. Paris: Seuil, 1984. *The Rustle of Language.* Translated by Richard Howard. New York: Hill and Wang, 1986.

Incidents. Paris: Seuil, 1987.

Books and Special Issues on Roland Barthes

Heath, Stephen. *Vertige du déplacement: Lecture de Barthes.* Paris: Fayard, 1974.

Patrizi, Giorgio. *Roland Barthes o le peripezie della semiologia*. Rome: Istituto dell'Enciclopedia Italiana, 1977.

Lavers, Annette. *Roland Barthes: Structuralism and After*. Cambridge, Mass.: Harvard University Press, 1982.

"Roland Barthes," *Critique* 423–24 (August–September 1982).

"Roland Barthes," *L'Esprit créateur* 22 (Fall 1982).

Culler, Jonathan. *Barthes*. New York: Oxford University Press, 1983.

Ungar, Steven. *Roland Barthes: The Professor of Desire*. Lincoln: University of Nebraska Press, 1983.

Roger, Philippe. *Roland Barthes, roman*. Paris: Grasset, "Figures," 1986.

Other Works Cited

Baudelaire, Charles. *Œuvres complètes*. Éditées par Claude Pichois. 2 vols. Paris: Gallimard, "Bibliothèque de la Pléiade," 1975–76.

Benjamin, Walter. *Briefe*. Herausgegeben und mit Ammerkungen versehen von Gershom Sholem und Theodor W. Adorno. 2 vols. Frankfurt am Main: Suhrkamp Verlag, 1966.

———. *Illuminations*. Edited, with an introduction, by Hannah Arendt and translated by Harry Zohn. New York: Schocken Books, 1969.

———. *Reflections*. Edited, with an introduction, by Peter Demetz and translated by Edmund Jephcott. New York: Schocken Books, 1986.

Benveniste, Émile. *Problèmes de linguistique générale*. 2 vols. Paris: Gallimard, 1966–74.

Blanchot, Maurice. *L'Espace littéraire*. Paris: Gallimard, 1955. Reprint. Paris: Gallimard, "Idées," 1968. *The Space of Literature*. Translated by Ann Smock. Lincoln: University of Nebraska Press, 1982.

———. *Le Livre à venir*. Paris: Gallimard, 1959. Reprint. Paris: Gallimard, "Idées," 1971.

———. *La Folie du jour*. Montpellier: Fata Morgana, 1973.

———. *Le Pas au-delà*. Paris: Gallimard, 1973.

———. *The Sirens' Song: Selected Essays*. Edited, with an introduction, by Gabriel Josipovici and translated by Sacha Rabinovitch. Bloomington: Indiana University Press, 1982.

———. *"The Gaze of Orpheus," and Other Literary Essays*. Edited, with an afterword, by P. Adam Sitney and translated by Lydia Davis; foreword by Geoffrey Hartman. Barrytown, N.Y.: Station Hill Press, 1981.

Camus, Albert. *Essais*. Notes et variantes par Roger Quilliot et Louis Faucon. Paris: Gallimard, "Bibliothèque de la Pléiade," 1965.

Compagnon, Antoine. *La Troisième République des lettres, de Flaubert à Proust*. Paris: Seuil, 1983.

Crouzet, Michel. *Stendhal et la langage*. Paris: Gallimard, 1981.

Derrida, Jacques. *De la grammatologie*. Paris: Minuit, "Critique," 1967. *Of*

Grammatology. Translated by Gayatri Chakravorty Spivak. Baltimore, Md.: Johns Hopkins University Press, 1976.

Febvre, Lucien. "La Sensibilité et l'histoire: Comment reconstituer la vie affective d'autrefois?" *Annales* 1–2 (January–June 1941), pp. 5–20.

———. *Le Problème de l'incroyance au seizième siècle: La Religion de Rabelais*. Paris: Albin Michel, 1942. *The Problem of Unbelief in the Sixteenth Century: The Religion of Rabelais*. Translated by Beatrice Gottlieb. Cambridge, Mass.: Harvard University Press, 1982.

———. *Michelet*. Geneva and Paris: Trois Collines, 1946.

———. *A New Kind of History: From the Writings of Lucien Febvre*. Edited by Peter Burke and translated by K. Folca. London: Routledge and Kegan Paul, 1973.

Flaubert, Gustave. *Œuvres complètes: Correspondance*. 12 vols. Paris: Conard, 1926–54. *The Letters of Gustave Flaubert (1830–1857)*. Selected, edited, and translated by Francis Steegmuller. Cambridge, Mass.: Harvard University Press, 1980.

Fontanier, Pierre. *Les Figures du discours*. Introduction by Gérard Genette. Paris: Flammarion, 1977.

Foucault, Michel. *Histoire de la folie à l'âge classique*. Paris: Plon, 1961. Augmented reprint. Paris: Gallimard, 1972. *Madness and Civilization*. Translated by Richard Howard. New York: Pantheon Books, 1965. Reprint. New York: Vintage Books, 1973.

———. *Naissance de la clinique*. Paris: Presses universitaires de France, 1963. *The Birth of the Clinic: An Archeology of Medical Perception*. Translated by A. M. Sheridan Smith. London: Tavistock, 1973.

———. *Surveiller et punir*. Paris: Gallimard, 1975. *Discipline and Punish: The Birth of the Prison*. Translated by Alan Sheridan. London: Penguin Books, 1977.

Gadamer, Hans Georg. *Truth and Method*. Edited by Garrett Barden and John Cumming. New York: Seabury Press, 1975.

Genette, Gérard. *Figures I*. Paris: Seuil, 1966. Reprint. Paris: Seuil, "Points," 1976.

Habermas, Jürgen. *Legitimation Crisis*. Translated by Thomas McCarthy. Boston: Beacon Press, 1975.

———. *Communication and the Evolution of Society*. Translated, with an introduction, by Thomas McCarthy. Boston: Beacon Press, 1979.

———. *The Theory of Communicative Action*. Translated by Thomas McCarthy. Boston: Beacon Press, 1984.

Hofmannsthal, Hugo von. *Prosa*. 4 vols. In *Gesammelte Werke in Einzelansgaben*. Stockholm: Berman-Fischer, 1950–55.

———. *Selected Prose*. Translated by Marry Hottinger, Tania Stern, and James Stern; introduction by Hermann Broch. New York: Pantheon Books, 1952.

Jaspers, Karl. *Strindberg et Van Gogh, Hölderlin et Swedenborg*. Traduit par Hélène Naef; précédé d'une étude de Maurice Blanchot. Paris: Minuit, 1953.

Lacan, Jacques. *Écrits*. Paris: Seuil, 1966. *Écrits: A Selection*. Translated by Alan Sheridan. New York: Norton, 1977.

Lanson, Gustave. *Méthodes de l'histoire littéraire*. Paris: Les Belles Lettres, 1925.

Michelet, Jules. *La Sorcière*. Paris: Julliard, 1964. *Satanism and Witchcraft: A Study in Medieval Superstition*. Translated by A. R. Allinson. Secaucus, N.J.: Citadel Press, 1973.

————. *Œuvres complètes*. Éditées par Paul Viallaneix. 21 vols. Paris: Flammarion, 1971–82.

————. *Le Peuple*. Introduction et notes de Paul Viallaneix. Paris: Flammarion, 1974.

Nietzsche, Friedrich. *Götzen-Dämmerung. Werke 8*. Berlin: Walter de Gruyter & Co., 1969.

Perelman, Chaïm. *L'Empire rhétorique*. Paris: Vrin, 1977. *The Realm of Rhetoric*. Translated by William Kluback; introduction by Caroll C. Arnold. Notre Dame, Ind.: University of Notre Dame Press, 1982.

Perelman, Chaïm, and L. Olbrechts-Tyteca. *Traité de l'argumentation: La Nouvelle Rhétorique*. Paris: Presses universitaires de France, 1958. *The New Rhetoric: A Treatise on Argumentation*. Translated by John Wilkinson and Purcell Weaver. Notre Dame, Ind.: University of Notre Dame Press, 1969.

Proust, Marcel. *A la recherche du temps perdu*. 3 vols. Paris: Gallimard, "Bibliothèque de la Pléiade," 1954. *Remembrance of Things Past*. Translated by C. K. Scott Montcrieff and Terence Kilmartin. 3 vols. New York: Vintage Books, 1982.

————. *Contre Sainte-Beuve*. Paris: Gallimard, "Bibliothèque de la Pléiade," 1971.

Richard, Jean-Pierre. *Poésie et profondeur*. Paris: Seuil, "Pierres vives," 1955. Reprint. Paris: Seuil, "Points," 1976.

Ricoeur, Paul. *Temps et récit*. 3 vols. Paris: Seuil, "L'Ordre philosophique," 1983–85.

Sartre, Jean-Paul. *Qu'est-ce que la littérature?* In *Situations II*. Paris: Gallimard, 1948. Reprint. Paris: Gallimard, "Idées," 1964. *What Is Literature?* Translated by Bernard Frechtman; introduction by Wallace Fowlie. Gloucester, Mass.: P. Smith, 1978.

Saussure, Ferdinand de. *Cours de linguistique générale*. Edited by Charles Bally and Albert Sechehayé. 4th ed. Paris: Payot, 1949. *Course in General Linguistics*. Translated and annotated by Roy Harris. London: Duckworth, 1983.

Shapiro, Meyer. *Modern Art, Nineteenth and Twentieth Centuries: Selected Papers*. New York: Braziller, 1978.

Starobinski, Jean. *Les Mots sous les mots: Les Anagrammes de Ferdinand de Saussure*. Paris: Gallimard, 1971.

Todorov, Tzvetan. *Critique de la critique: Un Roman d'apprentissage*. Paris: Seuil, "Poétique," 1984.

Vattimo, Gianni. *La fine della modernità*. Milan: Garzanti, 1985.

Veyne, Paul. *Comment on écrit l'histoire: Essai d'épistémologie*. Paris: Seuil, 1971. *Writing History: Essay on Epistemology*. Translated by Mina Moore-Rinvolucri. Middletown, Conn.: Wesleyan University Press, 1984.

———. *L'Inventaire des différences: Leçon inaugurale au Collège de France*. Paris: Seuil, 1976.

Index

Index